japanese style

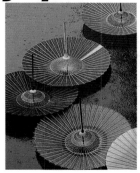
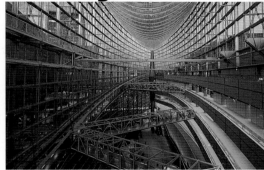

THIS IS A CARLTON BOOK

This edition published in 2008
by Carlton Books Limited
20 Mortimer Street
London
W1T 3JW

First published in 2001
Text copyright © Carlton Books Limited 2001
Design copyright © Carlton Books Limited 2001

A CIP catalogue for this book is available from the British Library.

ISBN 978 1 84732 043 8

Special Photography: Alex Macdonald
Mitchell Coster of Axiom Photographic Agency
Kenneth Hamm of Photo Japan
Executive Editor: Sarah Larter
Project Art Direction: Diane Spender
Design: Sue Michniewicz
Picture Research: Julia Ruxton/Alex Pepper
Production: Janette Davis
Printed in Dubai

CARLTON
BOOKS

japanese style

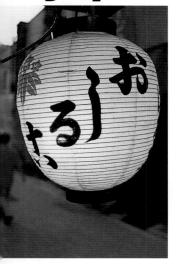
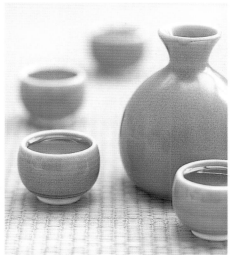
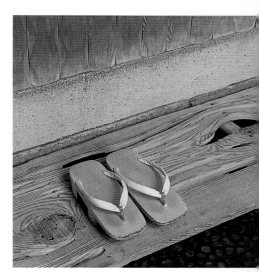

sarah lonsdale

contents

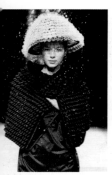 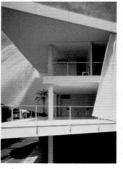 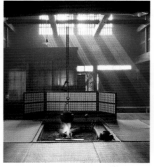 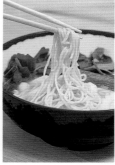 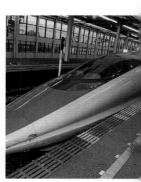

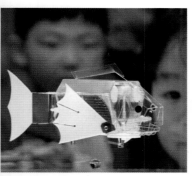

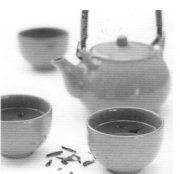

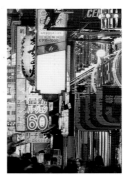

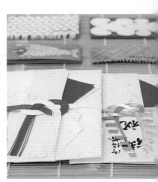

communication & packaging

advertising

homeware

products

6

transport

food & drink

interiors

architecture

fashion

introduction

Japan is a land saturated in juxtaposition, where the traditional world continually meets and melds with the modern. This long history of simultaneously adapting and distinguishing the native from the Western is a markedly singular Japanese trait. From the rice farmer in a Ferrari to young Japanese girls flocking to Harlem for gospel lessons, this fascinating contrast is also clearly manifested in a number of areas of Japanese design: fashion, architecture, interiors, food and drink, homeware, transport, products, advertising and communication and packaging.

Ever since Japan opened its shores to the outside world in the Meiji era in 1868, after almost 250 years of self-imposed isolation, it raced to catch up with the West. Modernization was synonymous with Westernization and the country grew at a remarkable rate finally culminating with the bubble years of the 1980s, which marked Japan's position as the world's second wealthiest nation.

Conspicuous consumption abounded and the Japanese travelled overseas at an unprecedented pace desperate to absorb all things foreign. The country's new-found wealth resulted in garish excesses. People dressed head-to-toe in designer brands, gold leaf was sprinkled liberally in sake cups and bowls of miso, while ice was flown in from exotic foreign locales to chill the *mizu-wari* (whisky and water) of Ginza's more fashionable nightclubs. By the early 1990s the bubble had burst and the country headed into a decade-long recession marred by industrial decline; the old Japan which had driven the country to riches was now suffering from financial woes. The country was also hit by a series of disasters including the sarin gas attack by a religious cult, the Kobe earthquake, and a nuclear accident. The days where the Japanese had felt invincible and secure had all but disappeared.

These disasters prompted the Japanese to question their values giving way to a maturity and self-awareness: the country was finally coming of age. Today, much of the framework that at one time defined Japan's social structure is in a state of flux. Companies can no longer guarantee lifetime employment and *giri* (a sense of obligation and indebtedness), which was once the backbone of the country's social cohesion is waning. In its place a new economy has emerged, one that is driven primarily by cost consciousness. Middlemen are suddenly finding themselves cut out of the picture as companies find more efficient ways of doing business. More and more young people are choosing to work part-time, while others are shunning large corporations and going into business by themselves. Younger women who may pay huge amounts for a designer bag are just as likely to bargain hunt for their clothes. Young designers are discovering clever ways to work with limited materials and although their work may be a little less professional they offer a greater variety of goods with wider appeal. Even Toyota, one of Japan's more established corporations has had to adapt to cater to the new youth market. In an unprecedented move for a corporation accustomed to consensus building, the company gave free reign to one of its young designers to develop a car with more youth appeal. Although the younger generation live an overtly Western lifestyle, sleeping in beds rather than futons, shopping at the Gap, and sipping café lattes from Starbucks, they have also rediscovered aspects of their own culture which is leading to a quiet Japanese renaissance. While at one time Western items were adopted and given a Japanese flavour, these days in a reverse trend traditional items from the past are taken and given a contemporary twist. For example the *yukata*, a cotton kimono worn to summer festivals and firework displays, has made a comeback over the past few years. Traditional

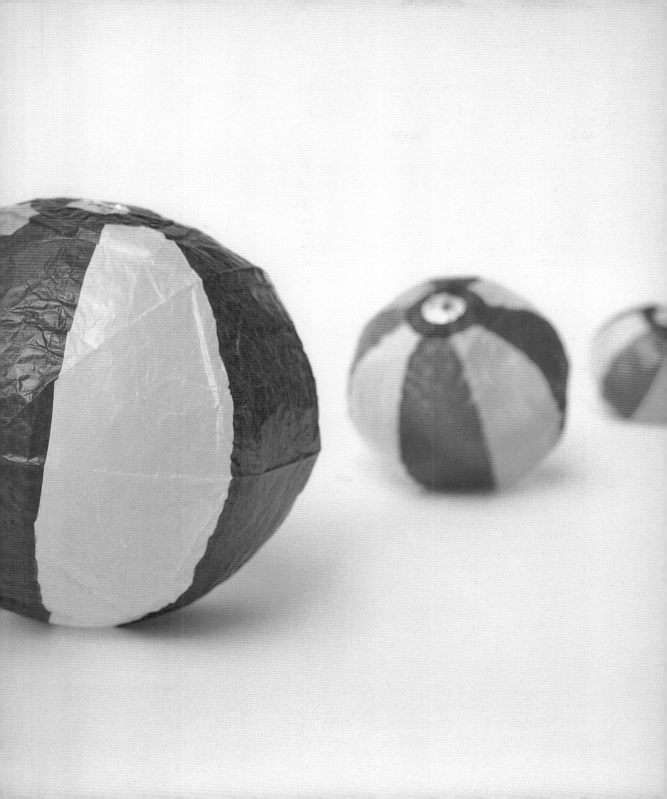

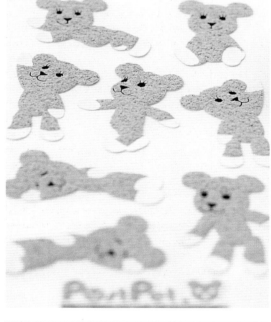

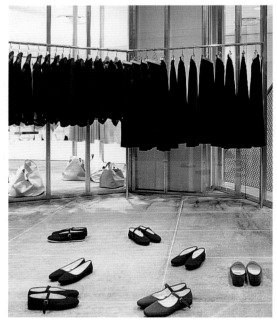

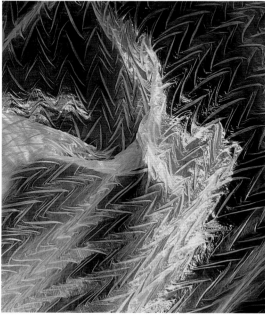

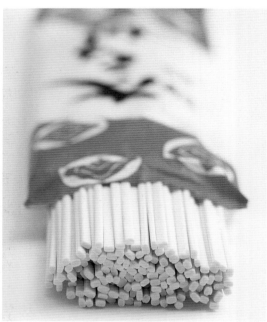

designs are now being worn coupled with more contemporary ones, and even fashion designers have started selling yukata in their trendy stores along side their t-shirts. Traditional wooden *geta* are still being worn on the feet with yukata though many choose to wear anything from platforms to flip-flops. Following a trend to hoist the yukata up at the waist like a mini skirt, the mini knee-length yukata made its debut. These days a yukata is just as likely to be seen in a nightclub as it is at a summer festival. Okura, a small store in Tokyo's trendy Daikanyama district, makes a hip line of indigo-coloured clothing inspired by Japanese workwear. They also sell denim kimonos, Gucci style bags in kimono fabrics and traditional *tabi* socks in metallic colours.

This renaissance is not solely confined to fashion. After years of knocking down *minka* (traditional rural houses) and replacing them with prefabricated modern housing, there is a new movement afoot to preserve this traditional architecture. In doing so, certain modifications are being made to accommodate modern conveniences, such as winter heating for the clay floor, yet maintaining the architectural integrity and organic feel of these homes. In the meantime, there is an emerging trend in the building of new homes to shun the use of plywood and incorporate more natural elements into the home, in particular returning to pure wood for floors and interior frames. The synthetic materials commonplace in prefabricated homes have indeed proved to be a poor substitute for the natural materials of past. Japan's traditional arts and crafts have survived through the handing down of highly refined skills from generation to generation. As modern substitutes have replaced many of these arts and crafts their perpetuation has been endangered. The young who have chosen to enter this laborious world have begun to realize that their survival depends not only on the continuation of their craft but also on finding ways in which these traditions and skills can become more relevant to contemporary culture without compromising aesthetic standards. Today much of what is considered traditionally Japanese at one time had its roots in another culture. A history of assimilation has created a cosmopolitan environment rich with foreign influence. The younger generation is able to use this international experience as means to inform their own culture, both adapting and preserving what is quintessentially Japanese, while making it more appropriate for contemporary living.

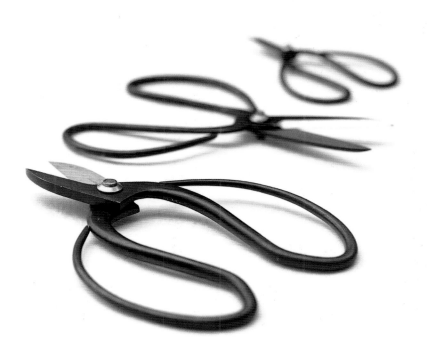

communication & packaging

advertising

homeware

products

transport

food & drink

interiors

architecture

fashion

fashion

The Japanese are fastidious followers of fashion, picking up trends and adapting them overnight. While Japan looks to the West for inspiration, Tokyo has become the fashion mecca for the rest of Asia, its youth desperate to copy the young Japanese female population tottering around in their *atsuzoku* (thick-soled shoes) sporting dyed blonde hair. Once a nation of neat dressers with uniformly tidy black hair, Tokyo is awash with a new generation of style mavens with colourful hairdos.

The "social parasites", those who live off their parents and spend their income solely on themselves, dress head to toe in foreign designer brands, toting Louis Vuitton and Prada bags. In a tribute to cuteness, young girls dress only in pink. Men perm their hair in an effort to emulate popular soccer stars, and high school girls in their navy uniforms wear baggy white socks as a fashion statement.

Yofuku, literally "Western clothing", is a somewhat obsolete term as it covers most clothing manufactured and worn in Japan today. The word first came into use in the latter half of the nineteenth century when Western clothes were adopted by the Japanese. *Kimono* meaning "thing to wear", was also introduced at this time as a collective term to describe native clothing. The wearing of yofuku, particularly by men, proved better suited to the Western-style office furnishings being adopted in the workplace. For women Western clothing was a form of liberation as all the subtle nuances, such as marital and social status, that were revealed when wearing a kimono were largely absent in Western clothes.

Although many women own a kimono, there are relatively few occasions when they are worn. The coming of age ceremony when women turn twenty is when most don a *furisode*, a long-sleeved kimono, indicating their unmarried status. Traditional Shinto weddings provide another occasion where the bride is required to wear a traditional white kimono and a heavy black wig; this is also one of the few times when a man may wear a kimono. The majority of young couples these days, however, prefer the setting of a church or a hotel where a wedding gown is the most common form of dress.

In the early 1980s, Japanese fashion designers began to make a name for themselves in the West. Issey Miyake was the first to come to the notice of the Western fashion press, followed shortly by Rei Kawakubo of Comme des Garçons and Yohji Yamamoto. The showing of their abstract, highly textural, monochromatic clothing caused a sensation and succeeded in challenging the very essence

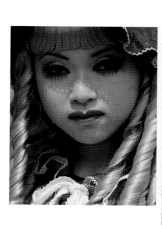
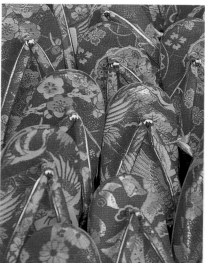
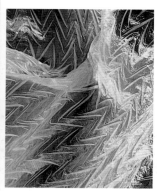

of the Western concept of fashion. Although this fashion triumvirate seems to shun the title of Japanese designer, their cultural background has enabled them to be free from the philosophy and confines of a traditional Western perception of clothing. Indeed familiar Japanese themes resonate subconsciously throughout their work. In particular, a reverence for materials is displayed by these designers in their selection, treatment and manipulation of fabric. Unlike the West where a fabric is tailored to the body, these designers let the cloth dictate the cut and fall of a piece of clothing, acknowledging the space between the body and the cloth and designing pieces that combine both functionality with beauty.

As the name, "Like the Boys" suggests Rei Kawakubo of Comme des Garçons brought black, androgynous clothing into vogue. Although in recent years she has retreated from the use of black, her conceptual designs still feature trademark *trompe-l'oeil* buttons and lapels, asymmetrical hems, frayed edges, wrapped layers, visible stitching and oversize ruffles. Her cerebral, deconstructionist approach to clothing continues to challenge the traditional concept of the female figure and her line of humped clothing has been her most progressive statement on the female condition to date, quite radical in its conception.

While Yohji Yamamoto is also renowned for asymmetrical, deconstructionist design, he manages to incorporate a level of softness, imbuing femininity into his clothing without pandering to stereotypical notions of beauty. His baggy cuts, misshapen lines, ragged hems, and tailored waists all share the same simple fluidity of form. Like the multi-layered Heian kimono, his clothes often hint at more than is immediately visible such as a different fabric at the back of a skirt, a hidden pocket, or a dress that may be zipped off to reveal further layers underneath. Like his contemporaries, Yamamoto's clothing is both multi-functional and timeless, transcending the temporal much like the kimono being worn for both night and day.

Issey Miyake has proved himself to be the ultimate pioneer in combining traditional textiles with futuristic fabrics. His early works integrate everyday Japanese materials – cotton, hemp and quilting – into contemporary design. In his "Pleats" collection however, Miyake revolutionized a traditional method of pleating by reversing the process, first cutting and sewing the fabric into shape then pleating it by machine afterwards. This reverse approach allows a material to permanently maintain its pleated or crumpled form regardless. Two-dimensional like the kimono; the "Pleats" line takes on new sculptural dimensions when worn. Miyake's continual pursuit of utilitarian beauty culminated with the "A-POC" line, his most democratic clothing to date. Though grounded in his Japanese heritage, Issey Miyake has succeeded in transcending cultural borders with his designs attaining that rare status of designer who is truly universal.

The only other Japanese designer of late to have challenged the legacy of Japan's fashion triumvirate, is the relative newcomer, Junya Watanabe, protégé of Rei Kawakubo. Colourful and conceptual, his clothing is still in a burgeoning state but his designs promise to continue a Japanese fashion legacy that constantly challenges our perceptions of clothing.

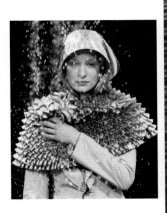
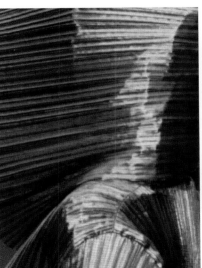
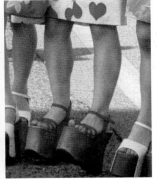

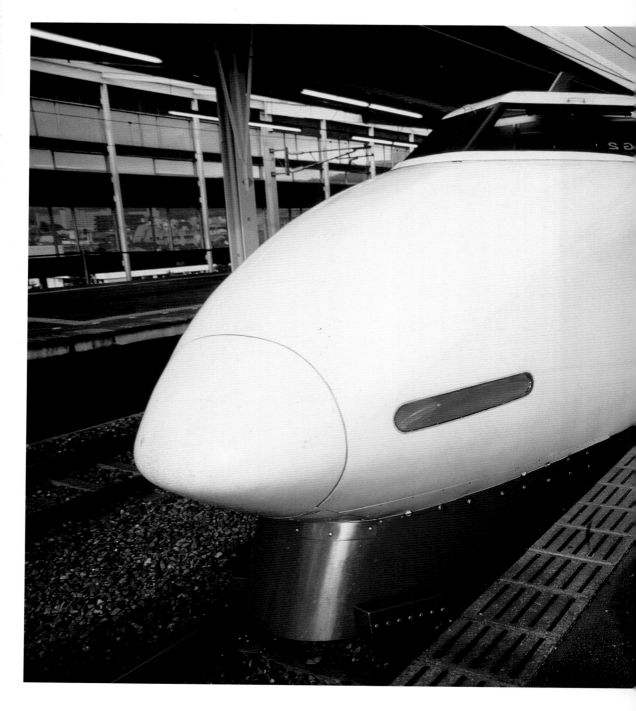

communication & packaging

advertising

homeware

products

transport

food & drink

interiors

architecture

fashion

12

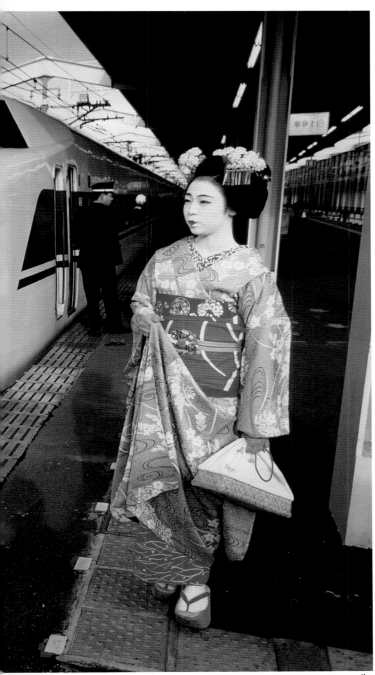

While Western clothing is tailored to the body with emphasis on curves and cleavage to denote sexiness, the Japanese kimono hangs straight, flattened against the body, the *obi* (sash) eliminating both the bust and waist. Like a neatly wrapped tape-free package, the kimono is worn wrapped around the body without hooks or buttons, and is tied with an *obi* and cords. Cut from a standard size bolt of cloth (the width of the body), the design is modular with little waste. the everyday wearing of Western clothes has relegated the kimono to the status of traditional art, like ikebana and the tea ceremony, with strict rules pertaining to its wear: seasons dictate the design, material and accessories to be worn while age and marital status dictate the type of sleeve. the *maiko* (apprentice geisha) shown on the left displays her youthfulness through the bright colours of her dress and her long, full sleeves. While the front of the kimono is folded high at the neck, the back of the kimono fully exposes the nape of her neck, one the most alluring aspects of a maiko – and in Japan, the height of sexiness.

maiko

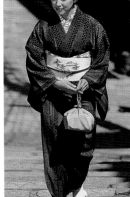

woman wearing yukata

communication & packaging

advertising

homeware

products

14

transport

food & drink

interiors

architecture

fashion

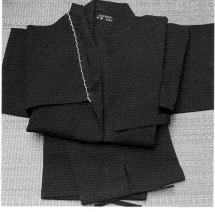

Japanese traditional workwear usually consists of two pieces of clothing, often baggy trousers and a kimono-like top that tucks easily into trousers. Like the kimono, workwear depends upon layering to keep warm and is typically held together with a simple obi or with ties, enabling easy movement.

Those who still work in the fields today tend to shun traditional folk clothing – despite the fact that it has now been elevated to craft status – preferring stretchy synthetic trousers and old fashioned Western-style aprons and bonnets. The head is often wrapped in a traditional *tenugui* – a simple cotton hand towel. Like the *fundoshi* (loin cloth), the tenugui is the epitome of Japanese design both simple in concept yet multi-functional. Tenugui are also used as a towels and handkerchiefs and are still popular.

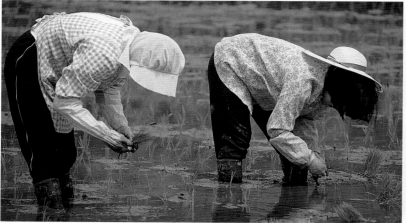

farming workwear

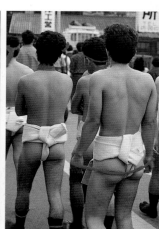

men wearing fundoshi

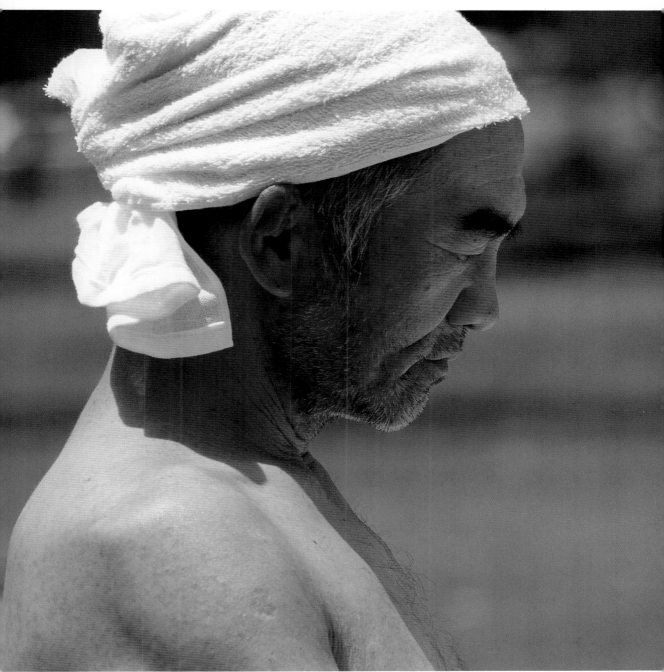

tenugui

communication & packaging

advertising

homeware

products

16

transport

food & drink

interiors

architecture

fashion

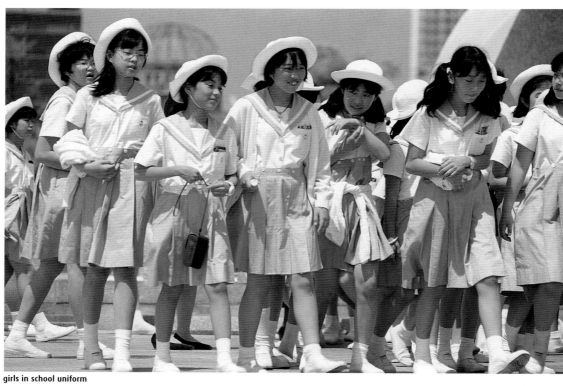

girls in school uniform

Japanese schoolchildren are readily identifiable in their neatly pressed uniforms: boys in black Mao jackets and girls in sailor blouses and hats.

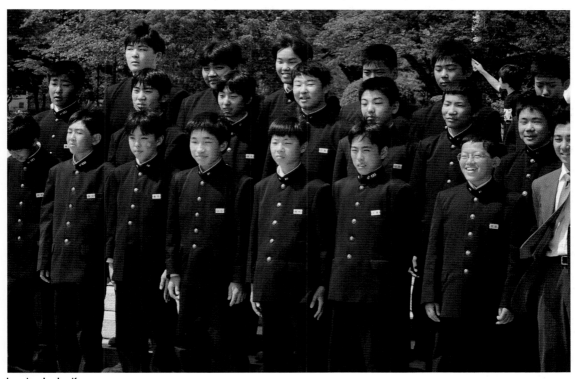

boys in school uniform

communication & packaging

advertising

homeware

products

17

transport

food & drink

interiors

architecture

fashion

communication & packaging

advertising

homeware

products

transport

food & drink

interiors

architecture

fashion

18

The hierarchical nature of Japanese society where language denotes the relationship between people (e.g. superior or inferior), is manifest in its love for uniforms. Ladies in pink tunics and matching bonnets sweep stations clean, petrol station attendants with striped uniforms neatly tucked into their boots welcome customers and toll booth workers in mustard yellow jackets and matching caps with black piping collect money. Uniformed workers give a sense of social order which the Japanese value. Even the salaryman has an unofficial uniform with his suit and tightly knotted tie. However, just as language is becoming increasingly less formal so are uniforms. High school boys now loosen their collars and ties while many salarymen are opting for a sports jacket over a suit.

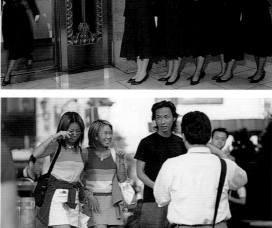

elevator girls in uniform

teenagers

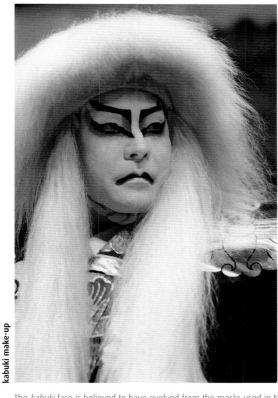

communication & packaging

advertising

homeware

products

19

transport

food & drink

interiors

architecture

fashion

kabuki make-up

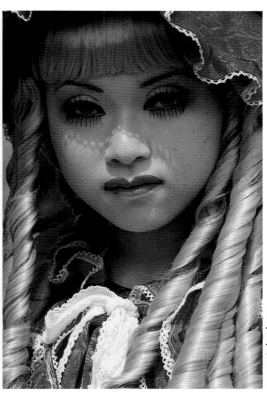

exaggerated make up

The *kabuki* face is believed to have evolved from the masks used in Noh theatre. The exaggerated make-up accompanies the highly stylized movements of kabuki. White faces have always been associated with the upper classes in Japan, those working in the fields being tanned by the sun. Geisha also keep their faces white. Japanese youth often incorporate a certain fantasy element in their dress: whimsical *Alice in Wonderland* outfits and cute pink ensembles do not look out of place in Japan's fashionable neighbourhoods. Just as in kabuki, make up often takes on exaggerated forms like the "Little Bo-Peep" look seen here.

communication & packaging

advertising

homeware

products

20

transport

food & drink

interiors

architecture

fashion

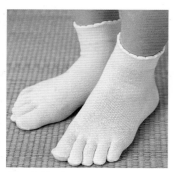

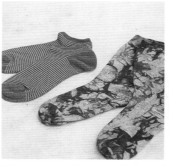

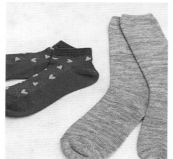

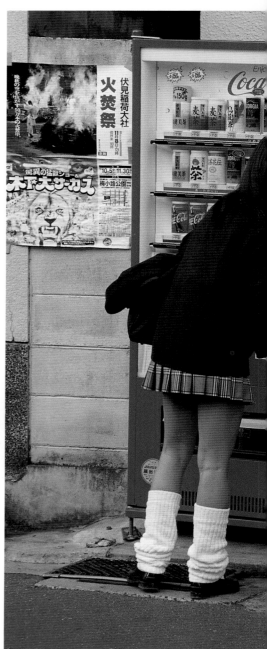

Shoes are removed in Japanese homes and in some restaurants and offices, so great attention to detail and design is bestowed upon socks in Japan. In the 1990s, socks became the predominant way in which schoolgirls rebelled. In lieu of the prim calf-length and knee-high socks that were compulsory uniform, baggy white socks that bunched over the ankles were adopted. The socks are held up by a special glue which has long been used by schoolgirls to keep their calf length socks neatly in place. This trend took off in Tokyo, established itself nationwide and is now standard schoolwear.

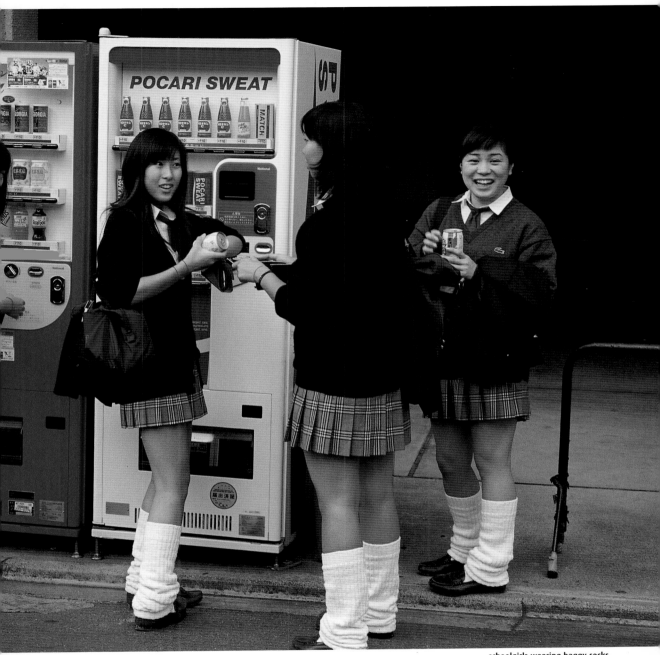

schoolgirls wearing baggy socks

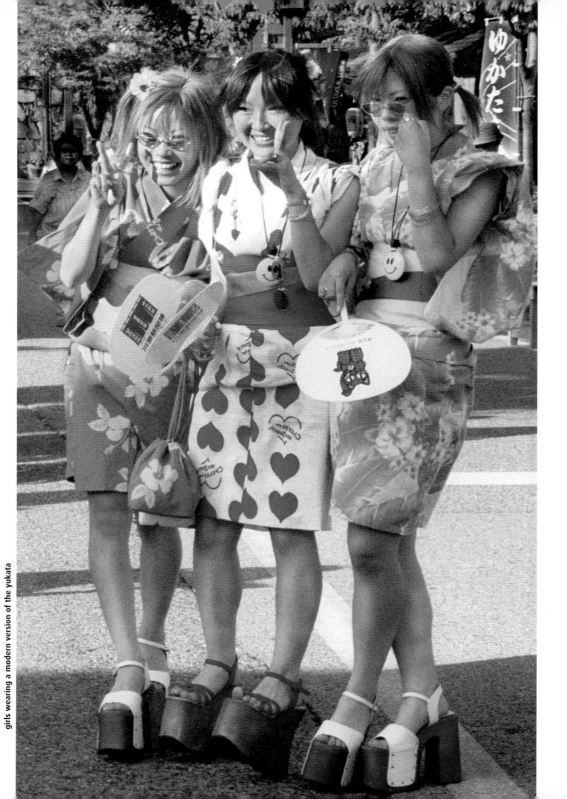

communication & packaging

advertising

homeware

products

transport

22

food & drink

interiors

architecture

fashion

girls wearing a modern version of the yukata

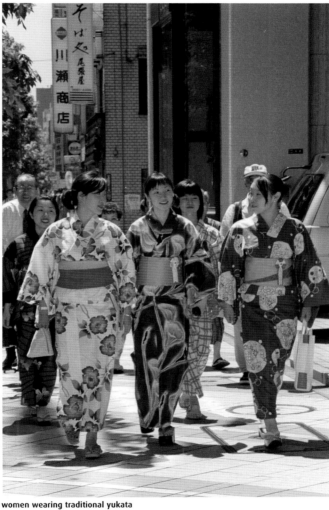

women wearing traditional yukata

Festivals and fireworks displays are highlights of the hot humid summers in Japan and it was once usual to wear lightweight cotton *yukata* on these occasions. For many years the yukata was on the decline but of late it has been enjoying a renaissance. Part of its recent appeal has been updated designs and styles. While the image on the right depicts traditional summer dress, the girls on the left sport fashionable designs, accessorized with sunglasses and contemporary Western footwear. Just as there were odd combinations of Western and Japanese clothing when the former was first introduced in the Meiji period, similar mismatches can be seen with the reintroduction of the latter among the younger generation.

communication & packaging

advertising

homeware

products

transport

food & drink

interiors

architecture

fashion

23

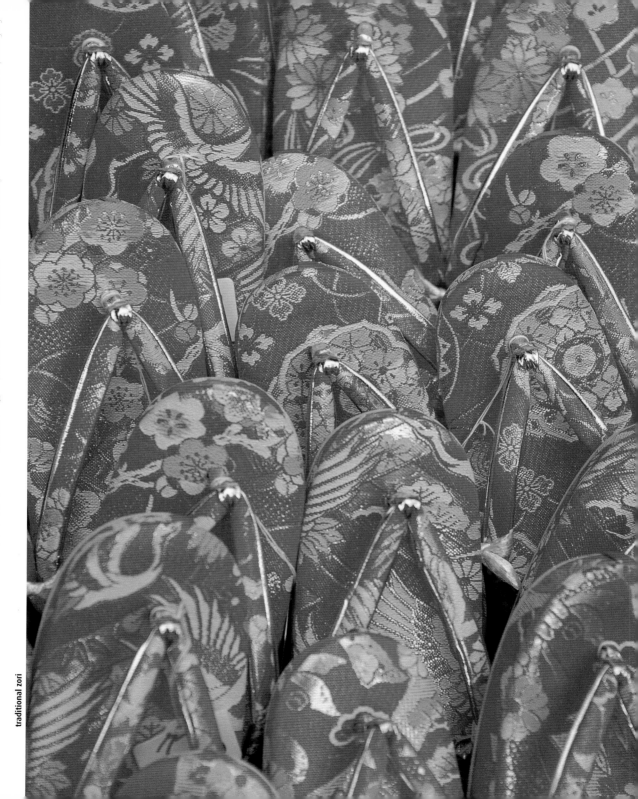

communication & packaging

advertising

homeware

products

transport

24

food & drink

interiors

architecture

fashion

traditional zori

communication & packaging
advertising
homeware
products
25
transport
food & drink
interiors
architecture
fashion

The straw sandals worn by the monks in the image below were at one time typical wear for farm workers. Made from harvested rice straw most families would weave their own sandals just as they would make their own clothes. The colourful *zori* shown opposite are traditionally worn with white *tabi* socks with toes and the kimono, and are easy to slip on and off. The more casual *geta*, made from one piece of wood, are typically worn with yukata although the new trends in yukata style have also seen thick-soled, modern sandals worn in their place. *Atsuzoku*, thick-soled platform shoes, coincided with what became the "Barbie" look in Japan. Teenage girls dressed in mini-skirts, dyed their hair blonde, tanned their faces and wore excessive make-up. The atsuzoku were worn in the belief that they made the girls' legs look longer and thinner while the high soles – often as high as 20 cm (8 inches) – added to their height. A spate of accidents, including broken bones and even deaths in traffic accidents by drivers wearing the shoes, caused them to be outlawed when driving. However, just as the Barbie look has been toned down, so the staggeringly high heels have given way to more comfortable soles.

geta

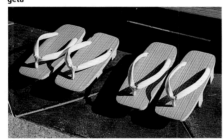

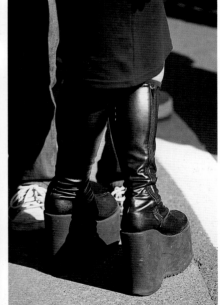

atsuzoku shoes

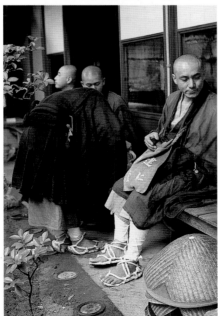

monks wearing straw sandals

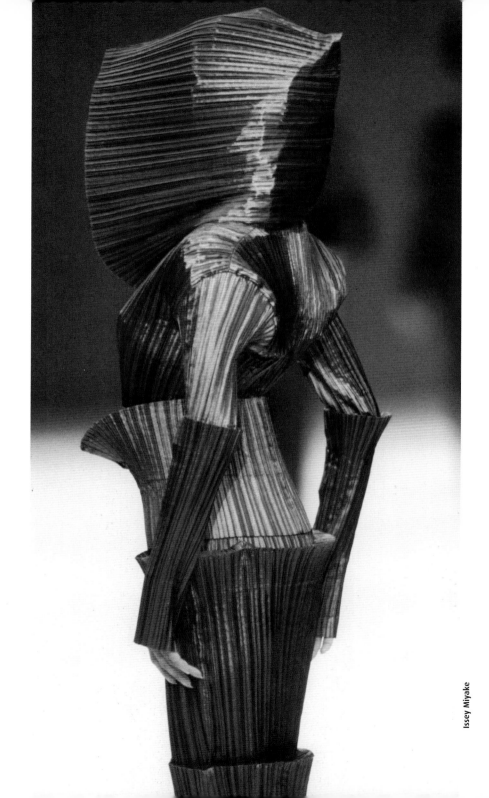

communication & packaging

advertising

homeware

products

26

transport

food & drink

interiors

architecture

fashion

Issey Miyake

Issey Miyake's early works as in the "East Meets West" collection, drew their inspiration from the world of traditional Japanese folkwear: *mompe* (baggy, workwear-inspired trousers), tunics that were wrapped over the body then held together with an obi-like tie and clothing made from a single piece of material (A-POC). As Miyake increasingly explored the innovative collaboration between technology and fabrics, his work took on more radical forms but were in fact grounded in basic principles of design that are inherent to the culture. The modularity, functionality and economy of space that form the basis of traditional architecture and product design are resonant in Miyake's clothing: a backpack that unzips into a coat or a dress that rolls into a small ball and remains wrinkle free and the A-POC clothing. Miyake's "Pleats" collection shown here resembles the two-dimensional kimono, which, once worn, becomes three-dimensional, taking on a new form as the material shimmers with the movement of the body.

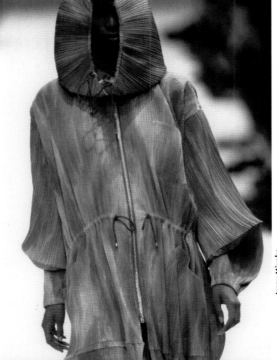

Issey Miyake

communication & packaging

advertising

homeware

products

28

transport

food & drink

interiors

architecture

fashion

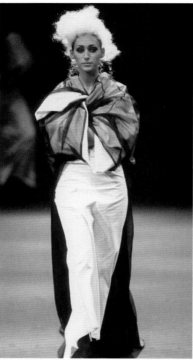

Comme des Garçons

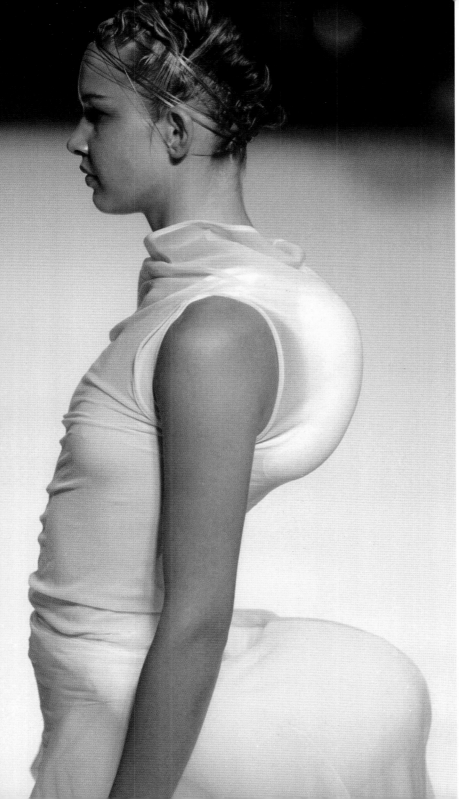

Renowned in the early 1980s for her design of a jersey replete with holes, Rei Kawakubo of Comme des Garçons has always challenged the concept of fashion. Her designs manipulate materials and juxtapose fabrics and textures, with layering and wrapping favourite techniques. Kawakubo subverts expectations by exposing seams and occasionally placing what is normally hidden on the outside of a garment. Like that of her contemporaries, Kawakubo's clothing tends to transcend age and time, exuding strength and confidence, it is conceptual and often challenging. While Western fashion tailors clothing to the body, Kawakubo's restructures the body in an asexual fashion. The distorted bumps in the dress shown here seem to be inspired by the hidden padding that is typically used to make a kimono appear flat and straight on the body. Kawakubo has taken this padding and placed it in an exaggerated form on the outside, totally distorting the female form and with it, our conceptions.

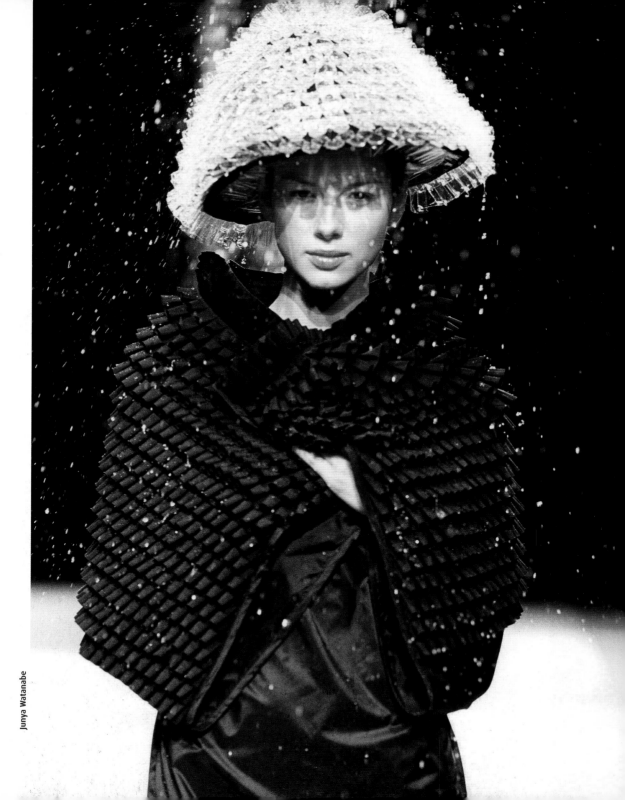

Junya Watanabe

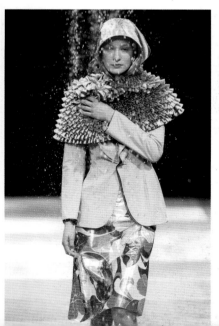

A protégé of Rei Kawakubo, Junya Watanabe has made his mark on the international fashion scene with architecturally inspired dresses using wire and thin pipes to fashion three-dimensional sculptures, while his recent collection featured finely sheared, multi-layered ruffles. Here a specially designed rainproof fabric was fashioned into layered hats and wraps, while dresses from the same collection revealed reversible linings. Watanabe's combination of the whimsical yet practical, echoes the work of Yohji Yamamoto (right) who often incorporates the functional with an element of romance and whimsy in his work. Yamamoto's recent Spring 2001 collection, mostly in black, sports his trademark asymmetrical cut but also features bags and hidden pockets sewn into the clothing.

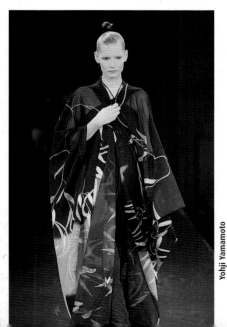

Yohji Yamamoto

communication & packaging

advertising

homeware

products

32

transport

food & drink

interiors

architecture

fashion

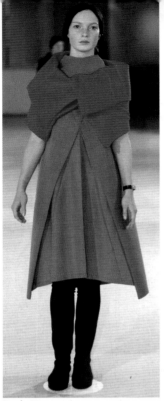

Kosuke Tsumura

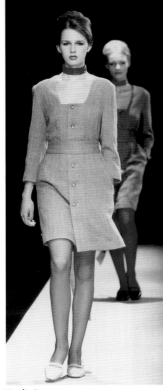

Kosuke Tsumura

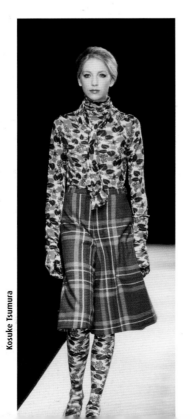

Kosuke Tsumura

Kosuke Tsumura is the designer behind the witty brand "Final Home" (an Issey Miyake subsidiary) which designs urban survival clothing and gear, such as a clear plastic coat with numerous pockets that can either be used to carry possessions or filled with newspapers as insulation to keep warm. Tsumura also designs a line of clothing under his own name, featuring a more soignéed look with clean lines and an interesting juxtaposition of fabrics and designs. Jun Takahashi is one of Japan's wave of new designers popular with the young. His designs draw on elements of the traditional yet are refashioned to give his clothing a futuristic flair, whether it be a Mao jacket meets *Star Wars* look or the pleats and plaid shown right.

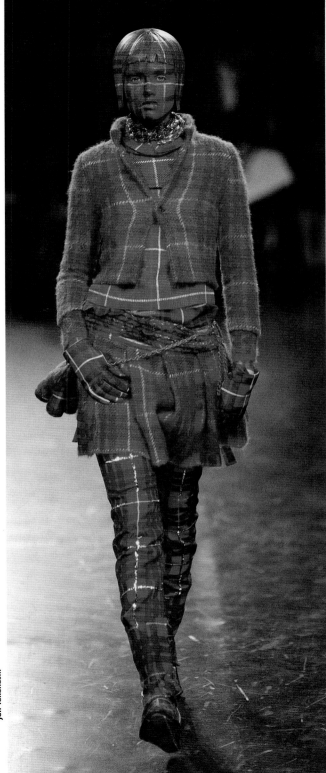

Jun Takahashi

communication & packaging

advertising

homeware

products

33

transport

food & drink

interiors

architecture

fashion

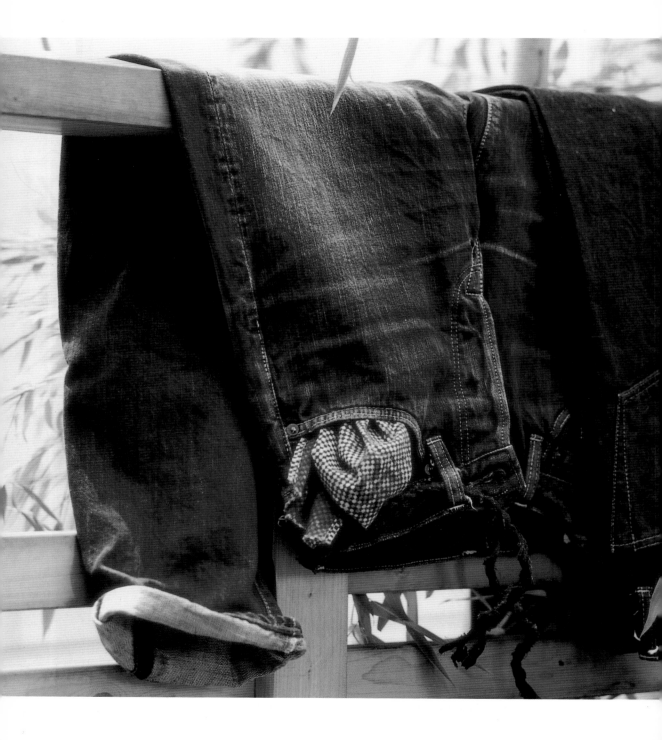

communication & packaging

advertising

homeware

products

transport

35

food & drink

interiors

architecture

fashion

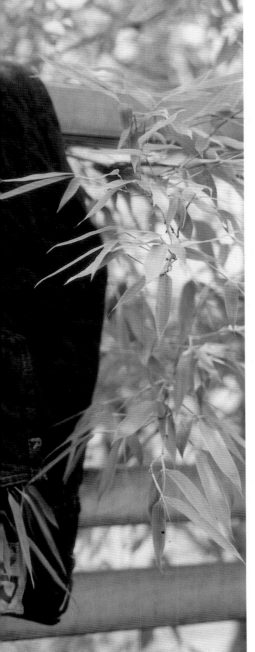

With a renewed interest in their heritage, a new wave of Japanese designers, including Badou R, are turning to traditional materials and designs for inspiration for their clothing. Aimed at those in their twenties, Badou R designs clothing with a contemporary appeal yet with references to the past. An indigo dyed shirt with tiny blue flowers looks like a Japanese version of the Hawaiian shirt. Plain cotton dresses display simple traditional motifs like cherry blossom, while skirts and tops pay homage to old fashioned folkwear. Many of the clothes are designed to be worn layered over jeans or with T shirts. Indigo bandanas, designed with traditional tenugui-style motifs, are symbolic of the shop interior which reflects a philosophy that values the design and quality of traditional clothing yet gives it new relevance with a contemporary twist.

Badou R (45rpm) clothing

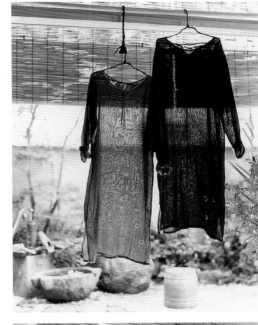

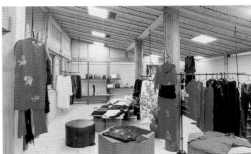

Badou R shop

communication & packaging

advertising

homeware

products

36

transport

food & drink

interiors

architecture

fashion

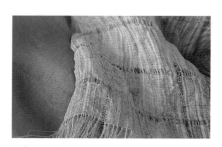

Japanese textiles offer a wide variety from the exquisite handmade fabrics by Chiaki Maki (shown on this page) to Nuno's highly manipulated materials that combine traditional techniques with innovative technological and chemical processes (opposite). Using hand-spun silks of differing consistency, Chiaki Maki weaves them into shawls, the tension between the silks producing a rich, variegated surface. She dyes her fibres by hand using naturally available plants and fruits such as indigo, pomegranate, madder and loquat, the colours produced reflecting the natural tones of earth and nature. Reiko Sudo from Nuno, on the other hand, takes a synthetic material such as polyester and subjects it to heat-treated processes imposing a permanent pressed or crumpled design upon the material. Fabrics are screen printed with chemical pigments rendering a multi-textured surface while other fabrics have natural elements such as paper and feathers woven into their body. Unlike the majority of Western textiles, those in Japan are highly tactile in nature and possess an integrity that ensures they are just as exquisite to the touch as they are to the eye.

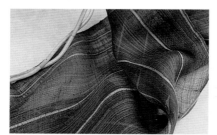

textiles by Chiaki Maki

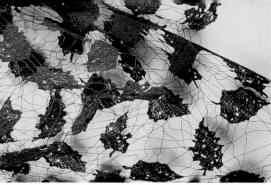
Fabric by Nuno: "Kareha"

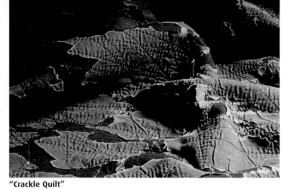
"Crackle Quilt"

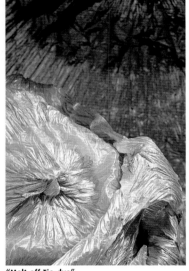
"Melt-off Tie-dye"

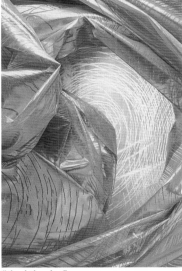
"Cloud Chamber"

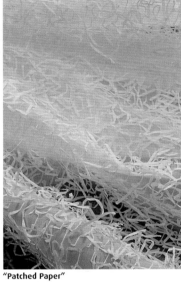
"Patched Paper"

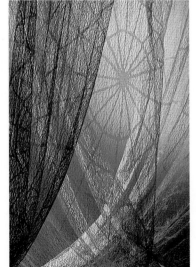
"Raschel Spider Web"

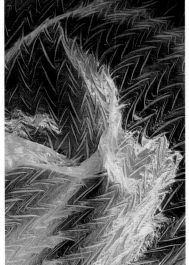
"Water Glass"

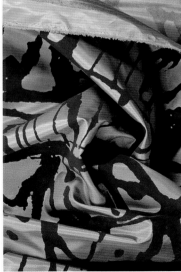
"Random house"

communication & packaging

advertising

homeware

products

37

transport

food & drink

interiors

architecture

fashion

communication & packaging

advertising

homeware

products

transport

food & drink

interiors

architecture

fashion

architecture

The image of a multi-storey building constructed from glass and chrome crammed next to a single-storey wooden house is not uncommon in many of the cities and towns across Japan. Such an image clearly illustrates the dichotomy that lies at the heart of Japanese architecture: the traditional versus the modern. Nowhere is this exemplified more than in the country's capital, Tokyo, with its 27 million inhabitants.

Tokyo is a myriad of skyscrapers, residential housing blocks, elevated highways, single-family homes, neon signs, monolithic high-rise office buildings and wooden structures placed randomly together in a labyrinth of streets and alleys. Unlike Western cities, with their spacious boulevards and ordered street plans, Tokyo evolved organically from a series of small towns. As a result, most side streets remain barely big enough for one compact Japanese car let alone a large Mercedes, a popular status symbol during the prosperous 1980s. The wider streets have pavements, a Western concept, but there are usually none in the smaller streets. The permanence of Western architecture that manifests itself in its planned public spaces with wide plazas and stone monuments to historical figures is mostly absent in Japan; the few open spaces that do exist today remain largely because they were once the homes of feudal lords.

Despite the sheer density of buildings, the speed of modernization and with it the gradual decline of traditional culture, a walk through Tokyo can still reveal neighbourhoods that retain the spirit of a small community. Housewives on bicycles with bags of shopping dangling from the handlebars mix with pedestrians and cars in the *shotengai*, the main shopping street. Usually located close to a train or subway station, the shotengai is the nucleus of the neighbourhood, serving as a local market and doubling as a venue for summer festivals. Loud speakers hanging from lamp posts frequently pipe music throughout the day some with a rendition of "Auld lang syne" late in the afternoon. These days the local *konbini*, or 24-hour convenience store with its automatic bank machines and internet access, an overt reminder of the country's modernization, is just as likely to exist here as an old-fashioned grocery store with produce stands spilling out onto the street.

Traditionally the Japanese have viewed their homes as private places with little entertaining at home. It is the streets crowded

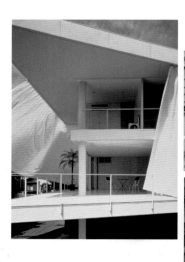
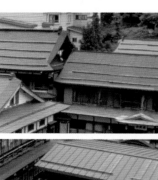
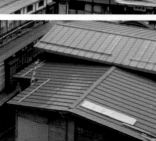
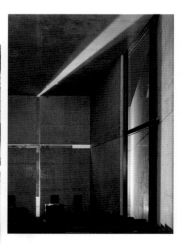

with people that become the public arena. A common sight is potted plants, often inexplicably in white polystyrene boxes, placed on doorsteps and lining the side of the road in lieu of a garden. While gardens in the West serve to separate the house from the street, these makeshift gardens become a link to the outside. This is particularly obvious in houses where the front door leads literally straight onto the street, only those wealthy enough to afford it, guard their privacy behind fences and walls.

The geography of Japan, marked by rugged mountains and volcanoes, has rendered much of the country uninhabitable. Villages cling to the sides of river valleys or huddle in harbours along the rocky coastline while the big cities have claimed the few coastal plains. The Japanese archipelago has a history of natural disasters that have made the Japanese acutely aware of the forces of nature with a consciousness of such instilled at an early age. The essence of Japanese architecture lies in its ephemeral qualities, its ability to renew and change over time. Traditional wooden post and beam structures lack the permanence of stone walls. Subject to a history of fire, earthquakes, volcanoes and landslides, buildings are not expected to last forever. In the last century Tokyo was wiped out twice: in the Kanto earthquake of 1923 and in the bombings and subsequent fires of the Second World War. Each time it was forced to rebuild. Unlike brick and stone structures with solid foundations, wooden structures once burnt leave no remnants. Building starts from scratch and rebuilding is a way of life.

This philosophy was particularly pervasive during the 1980s when Japan experienced unprecedented economic growth. Fuelled mostly by private developers and commercial clients, Tokyo became a centre for contemporary architects from both Japan and overseas. Old wooden structures were ripped down to make way for buildings of all shapes and sizes. As long as buildings observed zoning laws and the "sunshine code", a law that entitles a building to a certain amount of light, architects were virtually free to build whatever they desired with little consideration for the immediate surroundings. As land, when available, was sold at such a high premium, the tendency was to maximize use of the space rather than think in broader aesthetic and environmental terms. This accounts for the random juxtaposition of architectural styles. Steeped in ancient Buddhist philosophy, the Japanese may appreciate the traditions of classic wooden architecture, yet still their psyches are willing and eager to embrace the new. This absence of nostalgia to preserve the past has encouraged the development of some innovative and dynamic architecture and, inevitably, some architectural follies.

Tokyo can seem ugly when viewed on the macro level. Closer inspection reveals pockets of beauty in the nooks and crannies of its labyrinthine streets. The country is best reflected in the micro level, in the details of buildings and the minutiae of daily life. This philosophy is reflected in the work of several of Japan's contemporary architects who succeed in creating modern, fluid spaces with new materials yet are still able to embody the essence of classic Japanese style.

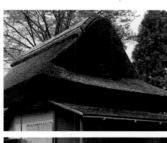

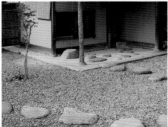

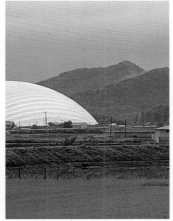

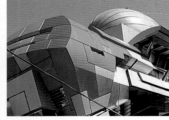

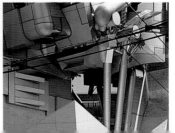

communication & packaging

advertising

homeware

products

transport

40

food & drink

interiors

architecture

fashion

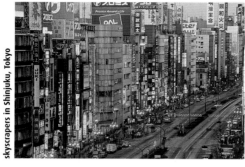

skyscrapers in Shinjuku, Tokyo

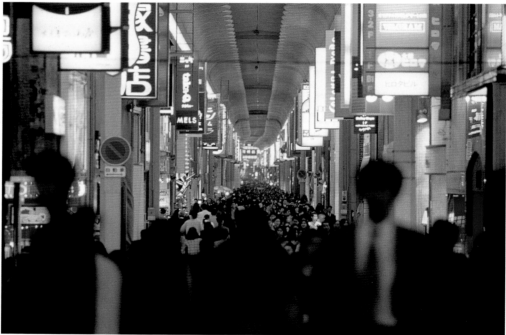

shopping mall underneath a railway station

communication & packaging

advertising

homeware

products

transport

41

food & drink

interiors

architecture

fashion

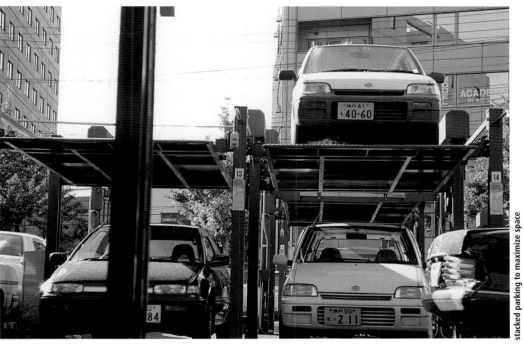

stacked parking to maximize space

The Japanese urban vista is a layering of buildings, signs, elevated freeways and pedestrian walkways. A crowded landscape with little available land means new construction tends to be vertical, expanding either upwards as multi-storey buildings, some only the width of one room, or downwards into the underground area beneath buildings. Solutions to combat urban crowding have been innovative: department stores are built around train stations and underground shopping malls link subway stations together. Littering the horizon of major streets are endless neon signs, some in English, others in Japanese, hung both horizontally and vertically. Mixed with large video screens, banners and billboards they provide a continual landscape of information and images.

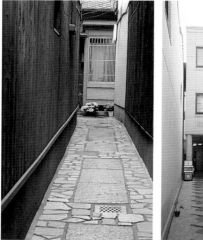
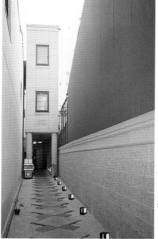

narrow alleyways between houses

Japan's narrow urban side streets tend to be tranquil in contrast to its frenzied shopping districts. Often too narrow for cars, they are used by cyclists and pedestrians alike. With restricted space, houses tend to fill the size of a lot with walls sometimes bordering the edge of a road, often only centimetres apart from a neighbouring house. Such proximity to the street means the conversations of passers by may often be audible from inside a house.

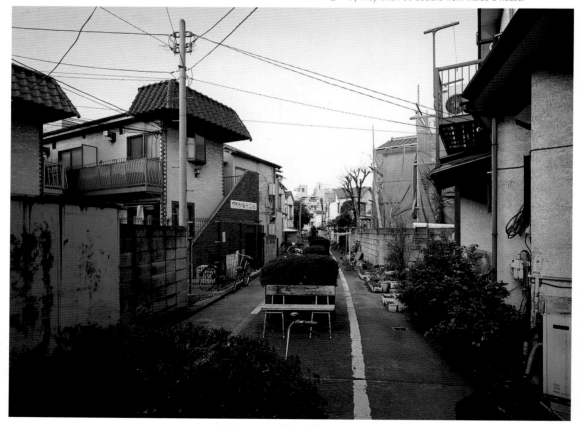

communication & packaging

advertising

homeware

products

43

transport

food & drink

interiors

architecture

fashion

With such constricted living space, life sometimes spills over onto the street. Bikes are parked, washing machines sometimes sit right on the kerb while washing hangs to dry on a pole outside a window. A love for nature manifests itself in the makeshift gardens often found edging the side of the road. Sometimes they can be as austere as one potted plant, but may also be a terraced series of bonsai plants built on makeshift benches. Small details such as the clear lower glass panel on an otherwise frosted glass door allow glimpses of nature.

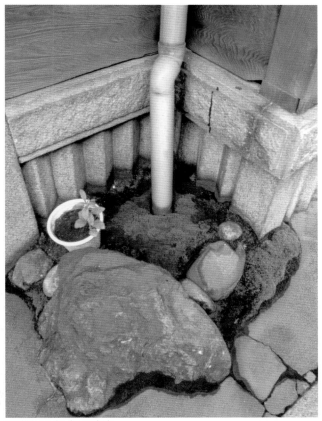

small garden by the roadside

communication & packaging

advertising

homeware

products

transport

food & drink

interiors

architecture

fashion

44

Modern housing has reclaimed some of the elements that have been particular to traditional design. Here, metal screens share the same transluscent quality as the bamboo blind, allowing light in while affording a sense of privacy.

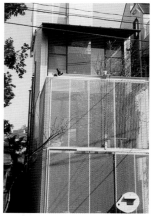

metal screens

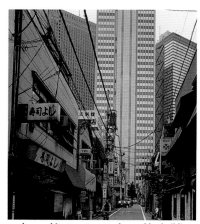

modern architecture towers above older buildings

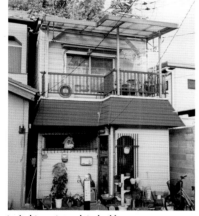

typical two-storey detached house

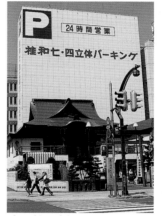

urban Shinto shrine

communication & packaging

advertising

homeware

products

transport

food & drink

interiors

architecture

fashion

45

Tokyo is comprised of several urban commerical centres that tend to mix shopping, business and residential living. A beer garden may be found on the rooftop of a department store, while a shrine may be located above a shopping mall or, as in this case, in front of a car park. In between these commercial clusters lie residential areas that are relatively quiet in comparison.

communication & packaging

advertising

homeware

products

transport

food & drink

interiors

architecture

fashion

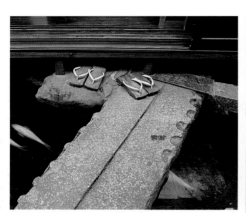

entrance to a ryokan – a traditional Japanese inn

46

Minka are traditional rural houses and vary according to region, yet all share the same natural, organic qualities and are perfect examples of how the Japanese have typically lived in harmony with nature. Minka were customarily built by their owners, relying on the help of neighbours and using local materials such as wood, clay, grass and bamboo.

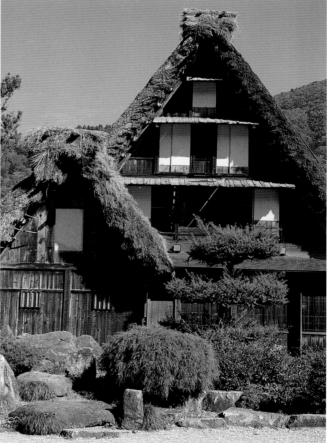

minka

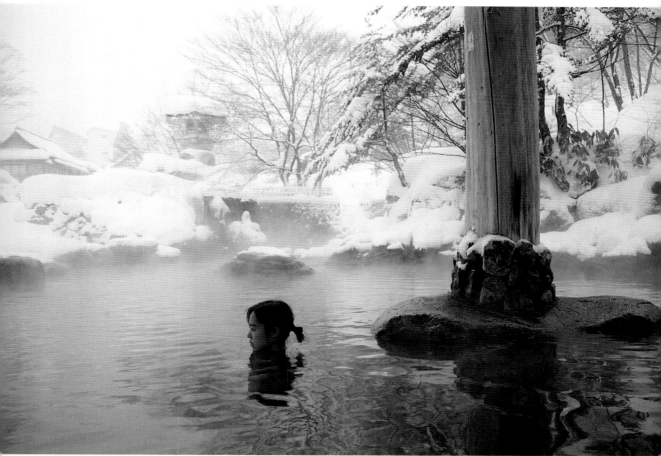

onsen bathing

Japan's volcanic landscape ensures an abundant supply of natural hot spring water and *onsen* (hot spring) bathing has long been an integral part of the culture and a custom that is still very much in evidence today. Originally an efficient way to keep warm, hot springs are now a common way to relax. Towns notorious for their healing waters cater to tourists offering a choice of bathing options, such as *rotenburo* (open air baths), wooden tubs or even hot water pools carved into large rocks.

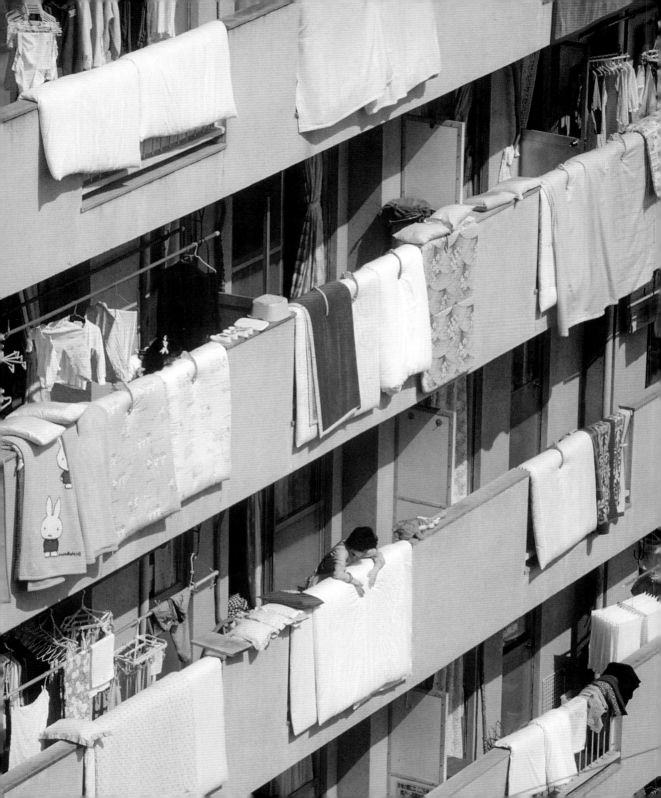

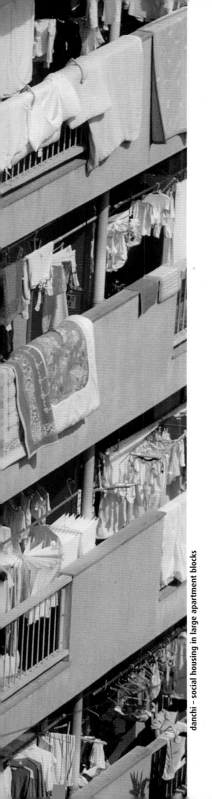

danchi – social housing in large apartment blocks

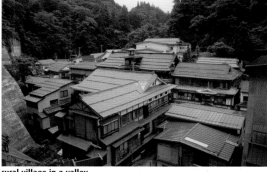

rural village in a valley

While urban crowding is the accepted norm, Japan's mountainous terrain offers little open space and life in the country can be equally concentrated. Villages tend to cluster in mountain valleys, with houses so close together that their roofs almost overlap, while the country's coastline harbours villages in their sheltered coves.

49

communication & packaging

advertising

homeware

products

50

transport

food & drink

interiors

architecture

fashion

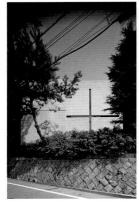

The quiet simplicity of Tadao Ando's Church of Light belies the subtle strength of the design. The grey reinforced concrete walls and a descending floor provide a backdrop for the shaft of light that enters through the cross built into the altar wall. The cross provides a link with nature while the passage of time is marked by the movement of light. Devoid of extraneous elements the focus of the church becomes the play of space and light.

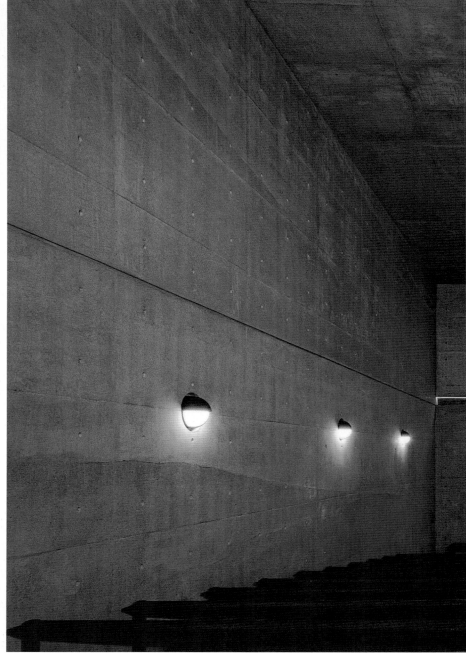

Tadao Ando: Church of Light, Osaka

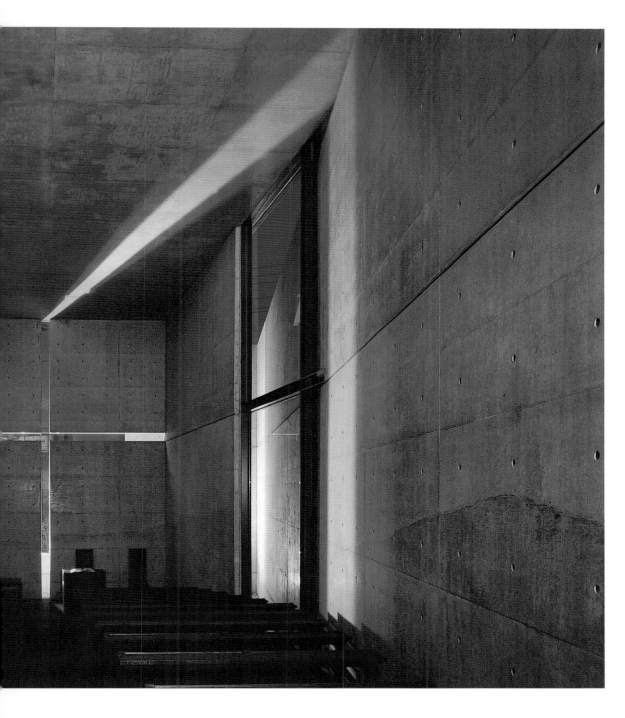

communication & packaging

advertising

homeware

products

51

transport

food & drink

interiors

architecture

fashion

communication & packaging

advertising

homeware

products

52

transport

food & drink

interiors

architecture

fashion

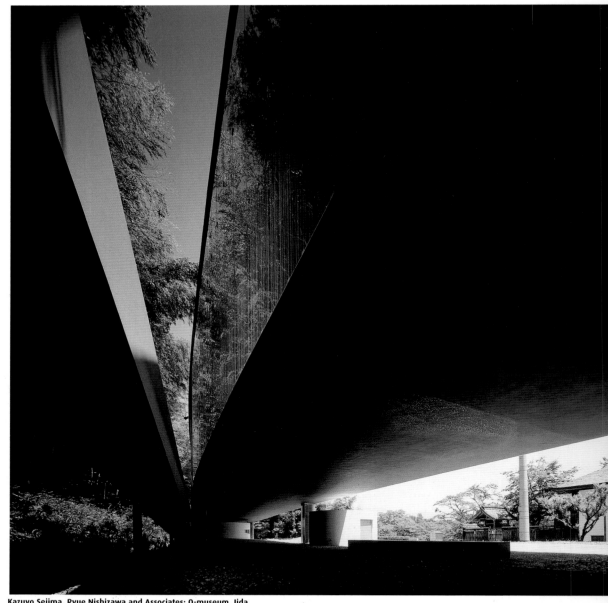

Kazuyo Sejima, Ryue Nishizawa and Associates: O-museum, Iida

The O-museum by Kazuyo Sejima and Ryue Nishizawa and Associates is located on the side of a mountain in the heart of the Japanese countryside. The elevated building allows visibility of the whole site including nearby historic buildings. Its rounded form emulates the natural curves of the mountainside while the glass façade reflects the surrounding natural environment.

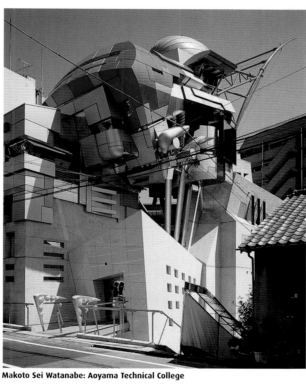

Makoto Sei Watanabe: Aoyama Technical College

The Japanese are accustomed to oversized images adorning the landscape: a giant gorilla hanging from a building, a replica of the Statue of Liberty on a store roof or a large Buddha in the grounds of a temple. Makoto Sei Watanabe takes this one step further in his design for Aoyama Technical College, where the building looks as if a large insect has landed upon it. The Japanese have always had a great propensity for accepting the new, however, built in the 1980s, this futuristic building has since come to symbolize the excesses of that decade.

communication & packaging

advertising

homeware

products

53

transport

food & drink

interiors

architecture

fashion

Fumihiko Maki's Spiral Building is located in Tokyo's fashionable Aoyama district. Its multi-faceted front with squares, rectangles, columns and cones and its multi-textured surface replicate the disparate elements of the surrounding buildings, such that it succeeds in blending in to its urban environment. The building itself is multi-functional, housing a store, gallery space, coffee shop, restaurant and theatre.

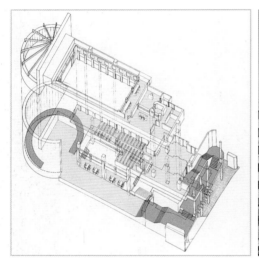

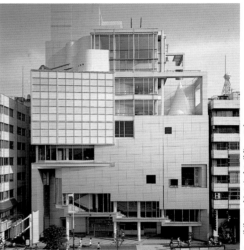

Fumihiko Maki: Spiral Building, Tokyo

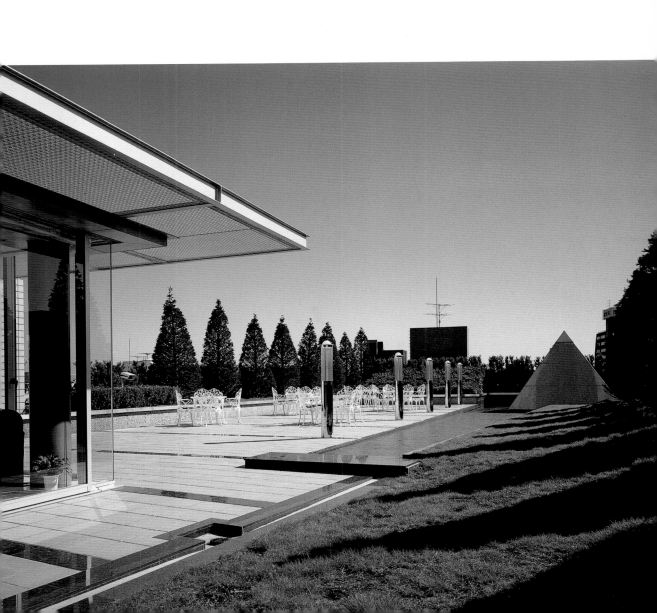

communication & packaging

advertising

homeware

products

56

transport

food & drink

interiors

architecture

fashion

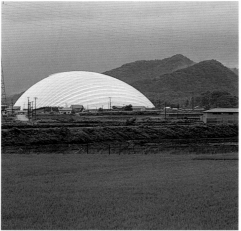

Toyo Ito: O-Dome, Odate

The O-Dome is a stadium located in Odate, in northeastern Japan. Designed by Toyo Ito, the large abstract white curve manages to coexist with the surrounding town and natural environment. Ito specifically chose local wood to construct the interior of the folded dome while its design replicates the shape of nearby mountains. Its paperlike form gives it a lightness and ethereal quality that belies its size.

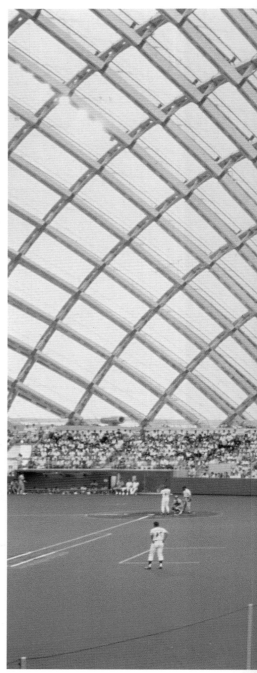

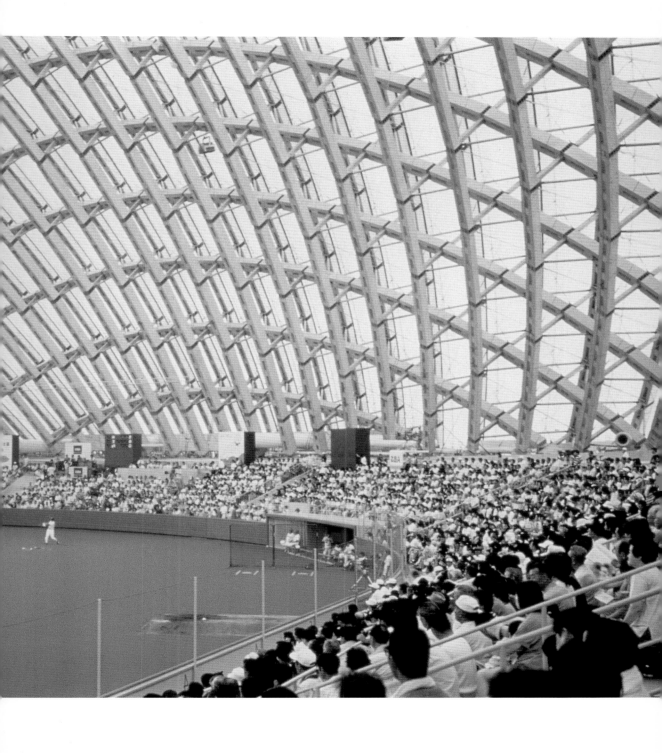

communication & packaging

advertising

homeware

products

58

transport

food & drink

interiors

architecture

fashion

Shigeru Ban has established himself as one of Japan's most environmentally conscious architects, best known for his innovative structures using recycled cardboard tubing. In his design for the Curtain Wall House he relies upon more modern materials but suceeds in embodying elements of the traditional Japanese home. Sliding doors are used like *shoji*, separating the rooms from the wooden *engawa* (terrace) area with the curtain the connection to the outside. The open design, sliding screens and curtains allow this house to expand or contract in a way typical of a traditional home.

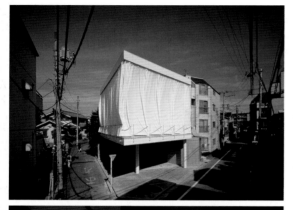

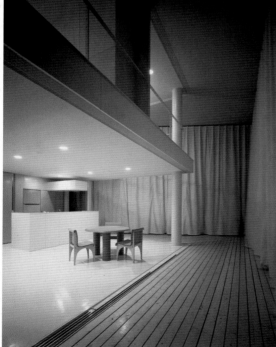

Shigeru Ban: Curtain Wall House, Tokyo

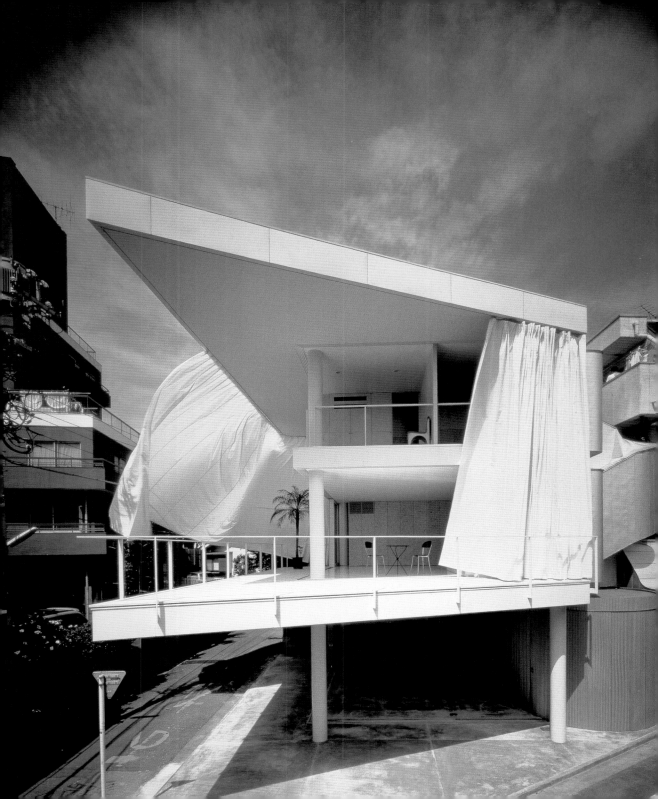

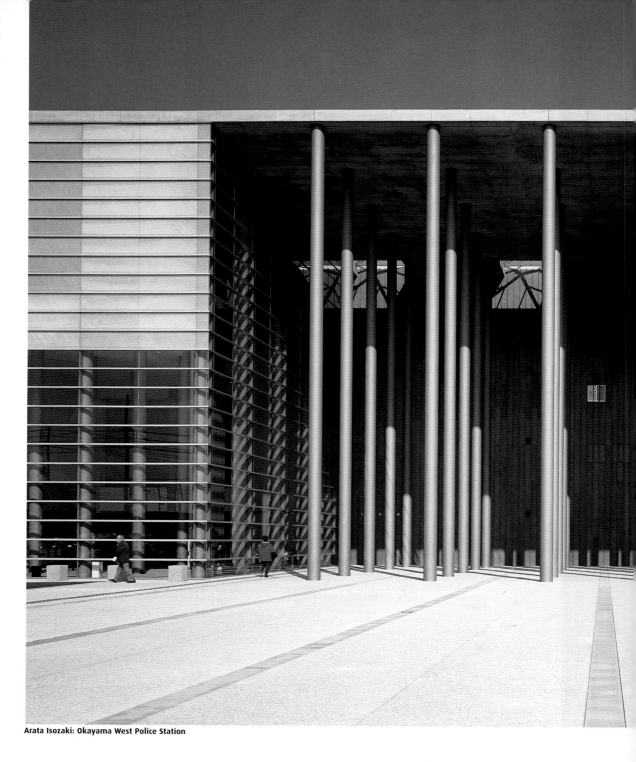

communication & packaging

advertising

homeware

products

60

transport

food & drink

interiors

architecture

fashion

Arata Isozaki: Okayama West Police Station

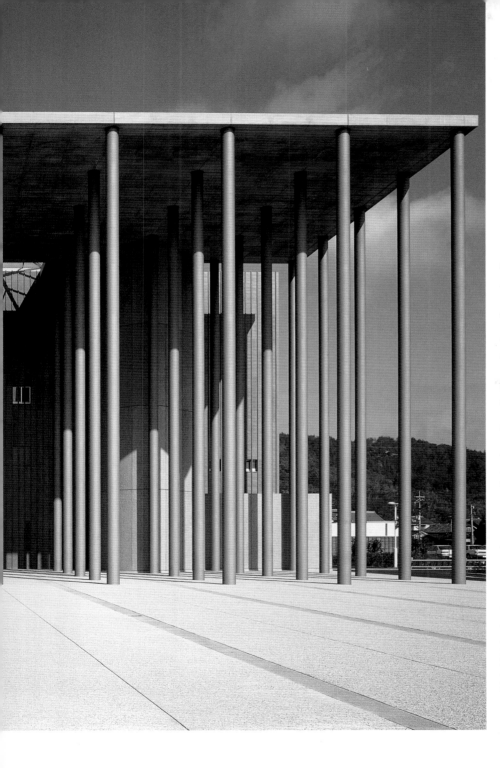

Arata Isozaki's building for the Okayama West Police Station was designed according to its different functions. The rear (north) side of the building is covered in zinc panels and houses the areas to which the public aren't allowed access such as police cells. In contrast the open south side is accessible to all. Isozaki's works usually feature weighty materials and here he employs narrow steel columns and a checkerboard façade of granite and glass.

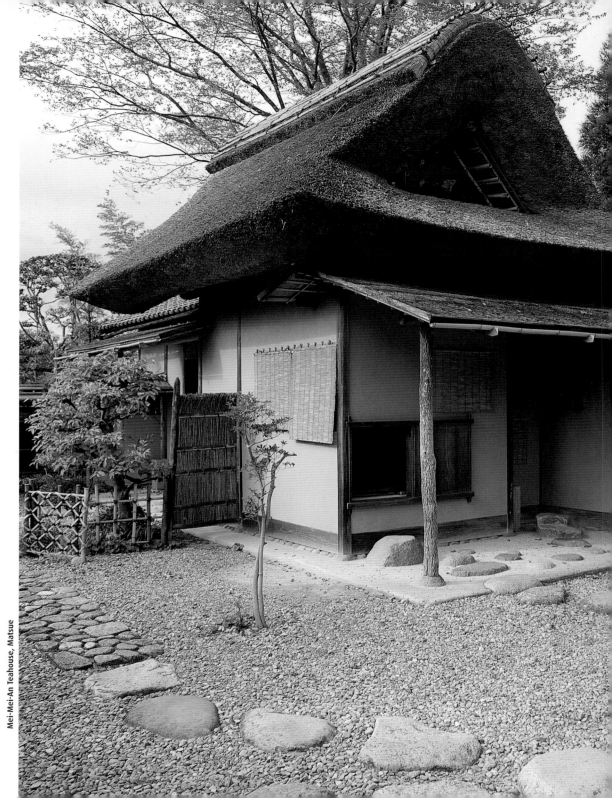

Mei-Mei-An Teahouse, Matsue

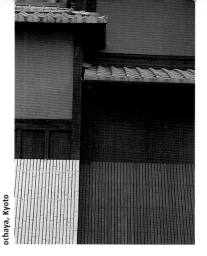

ochaya, Kyoto

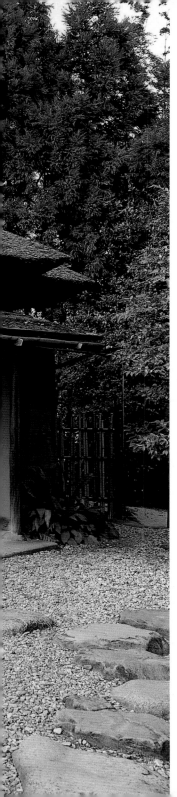

The *sukiya* teahouse is constructed with the aim of tending to both the spiritual and physical wellbeing of its guests. Guests approach the teahouse through a garden where the carefully placed stone path is purposefully laid out to slow down the step and help break the mind of everyday thoughts. The *nijiri guchi* teahouse entrance is designed to invoke humility in its guests, the small door requiring a guest to crouch then crawl through after removing shoes. The ephemeral is expressed through the natural elements used to construct the building such as the thatched roof, the large stepping stone into the tea room and the supporting post with its weathered bark. *Ochaya* (shown upper right) are also known as teahouses but of a different nature. Discretely shielded from the street, they operate like select private clubs and are most prolific in Kyoto. This is where geisha and maiko are called to entertain guests, spending the evening eating and drinking in tatami rooms behind closed doors.

communication & packaging

advertising

homeware

products

transport

food & drink

interiors

architecture

fashion

communication & packaging

advertising

homeware

products

64

transport

food & drink

interiors

architecture

fashion

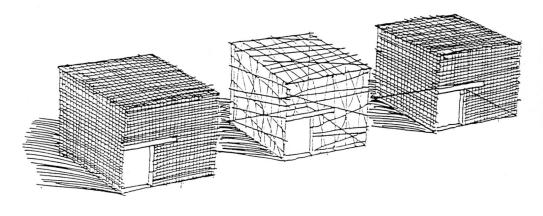

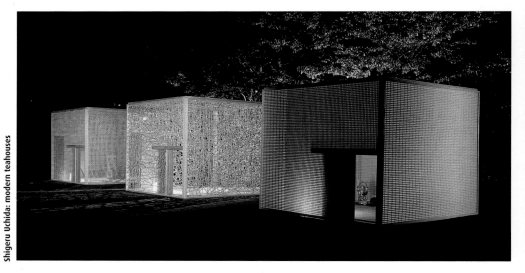

Shigeru Uchida: modern teahouses

Shigeru Uchida and Kan Izue have updated the rustic look of the traditional teahouse with their contemporary interpretations. While Uchida's wooden box structures are made from natural materials such as wood and paper; Pipia-an, Izue's teahouse, located in a garden on the roof of a building, uses contemporary elements such as aluminium, steel and glass. Both, however, are devoid of artifice and succeed in maintain the air of *wabi-sabi* (integrity and austere simplicity) integral to a traditional teahouse.

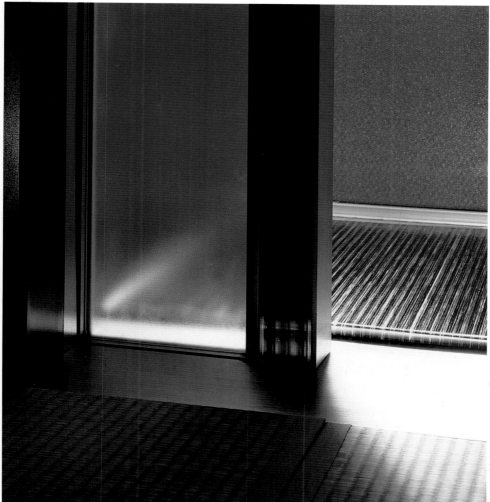

Kan Izue: Pipia-an tea ceremony house

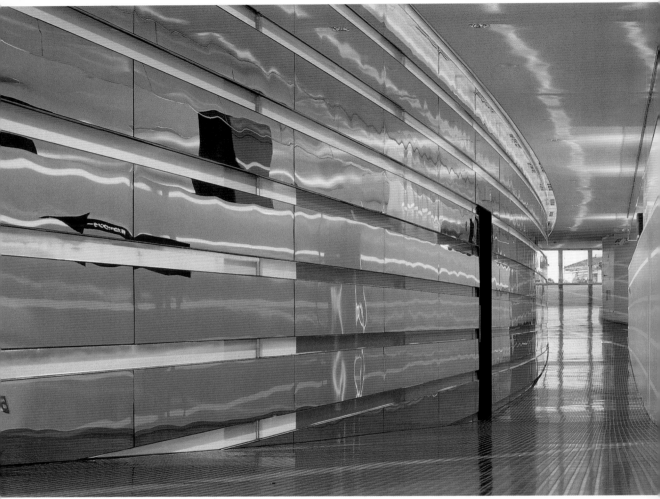

Kazuyo Sejima: Pachinko Parlour III

Typically pachinko parlours are garishly designed, neon-lit halls housing row upon row of pachinko machines, as seen in the photo of Pachinko USA, opposite. In a move to broaden their appeal to women, pachinko parlours have been been on a mission to update their image. In her design for Pachinko Parlour III, Kazuyo Sejima elected to keep the traditional neon but reduced it to a more subtle form and softened the space with a curved wall. The pachinko machines are still lined up in their usual form although a terraced seating area succeeds in opening up the space.

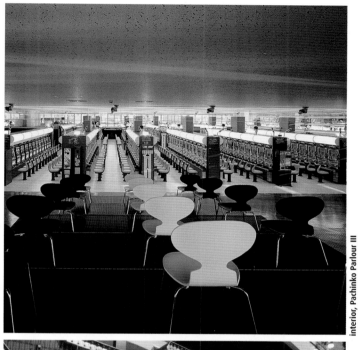

interior, Pachinko Parlour III

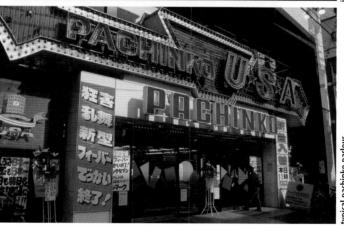

typical pachinko parlour

communication & packaging

advertising

homeware

products

68

transport

food & drink

interiors

architecture

fashion

interiors

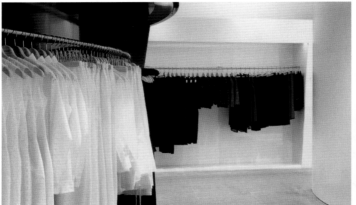
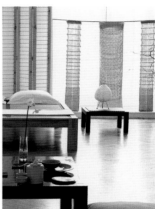

The austere image of a traditional Japanese interior of *tatami* floors, muted clay walls, *shoji* screens and empty spaces is little evident in the average contemporary Japanese home. The Japanese have been integrating Western furniture and style into their homes since the Meiji period. Initially, those who could afford to incorporated a Western room in their otherwise traditional house, replete with sofa and coffee table where visitors were entertained. Today the trend has reversed and it is often the Japanese style room in a modern house that is seen as special.

Not surprisingly, the biggest change in living has taken place in urban areas where well over half of the population of Japan now reside. Those in the country still lead a more traditional life, which is reflected in their homes: straw is used for tatami, while rice paper is used for the translucent shoji screens. *Fusuma*, removable padded doors covered with paper that slide across a wooden rail, serve as room dividers. Despite the introduction of modern synthetic substitutes, craftsmen can still be found using natural materials and techniques that are centuries old.

The traditional interior developed out of necessity and has much to commend it. Historically, Japan, as an island culture, was isolated from to rest of the world and was thus forced to rely on materials at hand for construction. Bamboo, clay, pine and straw were all readily available. Climate has also been a huge influence on design: extremes of temperature mean that Japanese houses need to be shaded in summer to combat the heat and humidity, yet insulated in the cold, snowy winter to preserve warmth. The shoji and fusuma can be opened to allow a cross-breeze through the house in summer, while an overhanging roof of clay tiles or straw provides shade. This remarkably functional and versatile style of interior lends itself well to accommodating large families of several generations that at one time used to live together. Rooms can be expanded for large gatherings then separated by fusuma into smaller spaces, which is particularly useful in winter when it is necessary to preserve heat.

With the exception of the kitchen and bathroom, traditional rooms are not allocated a function as they are in the West, but are flexible spaces that can be adapted to the needs of the dweller. At night, bedding is laid out on the floor while in the day people sit on tatami. As furnishings evolved, they remained minimal and were designed to be easily stored, such as tables with folding legs,

communication & packaging

advertising

homeware

products

69

transport

food & drink

interiors

architecture

fashion

zabuton (cushions) that are flat and easily stored. The only permanent piece of furniture was the *tansu*, a set of portable stacking wooden drawers with iron fittings and handles in which valuables were kept.

With the advent of industrialization, the population migrated to the cities where lack of space resulted in the development of *danchi*, housing developments comprised of large building blocks divided into small, identical apartments. Danchi are most prevalent in the suburbs of cities. The misnomer, "mansion" refers to smaller apartment buildings mostly found in the city. Here families live in a one- or two-bedroom "LDK", the initials referring to the living, dining and kitchen rooms. Over the years the multi-functional rooms of the traditional house have disappeared as Western-style furniture such as sofas and tables and chairs have become popular. The cleverly designed folding tables of the past have been replaced with permanent pieces of furniture that often dominate rooms and render already crowded living quarters even more cramped. What is most noticeable about a contemporary Japanese home is that, even with Western furnishings, living is still relatively close to the ground. Sofas tend to be lower than their Western counterparts and may well face a low table that has zabuton on the other side to accommodate extra guests. Televisions are often placed on the floor and beds, if used, are also low.

Despite rampant Westernization remnants of the classic interior have been incorporated into the modern home, some of it subconsciously. Glass replaced shoji for both reasons of heat retention and security, however, frosted glass is often used instead of clear, retaining the same translucent effect of paper. Many homes in mansions and danchi in particular are built with a main door on a corridor that is open to the outdoors. On the opposite side of the house there is usually a small balcony with sliding doors opening to the outside, allowing for cross ventilation. Futon are still usually hung out to air on a daily basis whether out of the window of a house or over a thirteenth-floor balcony. It seems some connection with the outdoors is essential no matter how restricted. Access the rooftop of a building and you may well find hundreds of bonsai being cultivated, a miniature garden in a concrete oasis.

In postwar Japan, the adoption of Western-style living was a sign of affluence. Ironically this trend is now fully reversed. Today, a classic style Japanese house or a designer built minimalist contemporary equivalent is only within the realm of those able to afford it. For the average city dweller, a visit to relatives in the country or a trip to a *ryokan* is the only way that they can afford to live in traditional Japanese style.

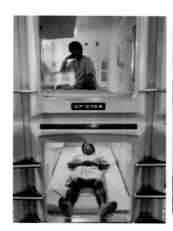
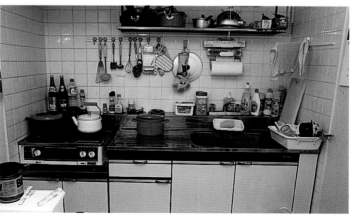

communication & packaging

advertising

homeware

products

70

transport

food & drink

interiors

architecture

fashion

A traditional structure is typically constructed with wooden pillars and beams providing the framework for a basic but flexible interior. Rooms are divided by *fusuma*, paper padded doors that slide across each other on wooden rails and may also be removed to expand a space when necessary. Natural materials are an integral part of an interior and reflect an affinity with nature. Rush and straw *tatami* mats are used for seating and sleeping upon, translucent paper lines the gridded *shoji* screens that separate the interior from the exterior while wooden beams are left exposed. The focal point of a room is the *tokonoma* (opposite). Designed to give an illusion of space, it is located in a recessed corner of a room with a slightly raised floor and a roughly hewn pillar of wood on one side. Within this space a carefully selected scroll is hung, a vase with an *ikebana* display will be placed beneath it and incense may also be burnt. All items are chosen for their seasonal allusions and are renewed accordingly.

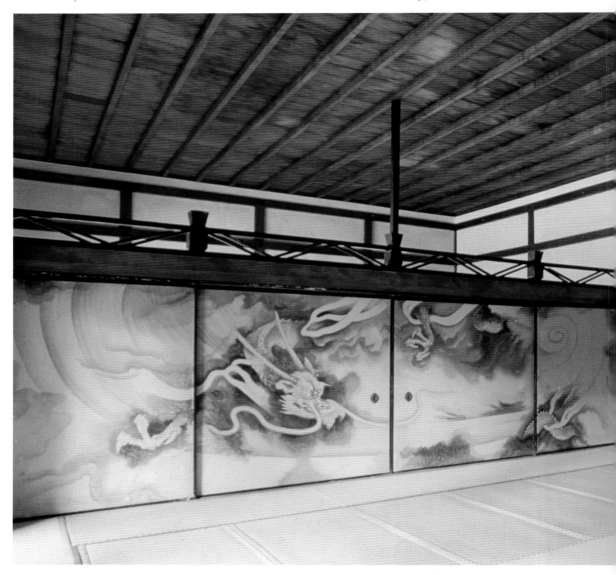

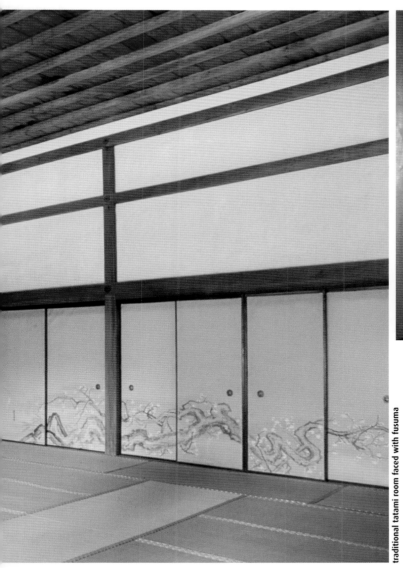

traditional tatami room faced with fusuma

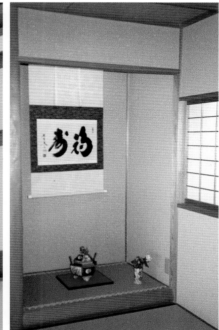

tokonoma

communication & packaging

advertising

homeware

products

71

transport

food & drink

interiors

architecture

fashion

communication & packaging

advertising

homeware

products

72

transport

food & drink

interiors

architecture

fashion

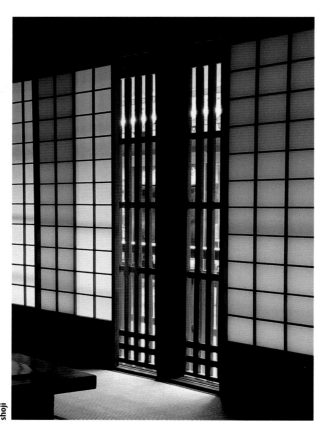

shoji

The natural elements that comprise an old-fashioned Japanese home or its contemporary equivalent, such as wood, paper, rice and straw, embody a certain tactile quality usually devoid in the Western home. Shoes are removed in the doorway and while it is customary to wear slippers in the rest of the house they are removed before stepping onto the tatami. Here the rush matting can be felt underfoot while the smell of new tatami permeates the air with a rather sweet fragrance.

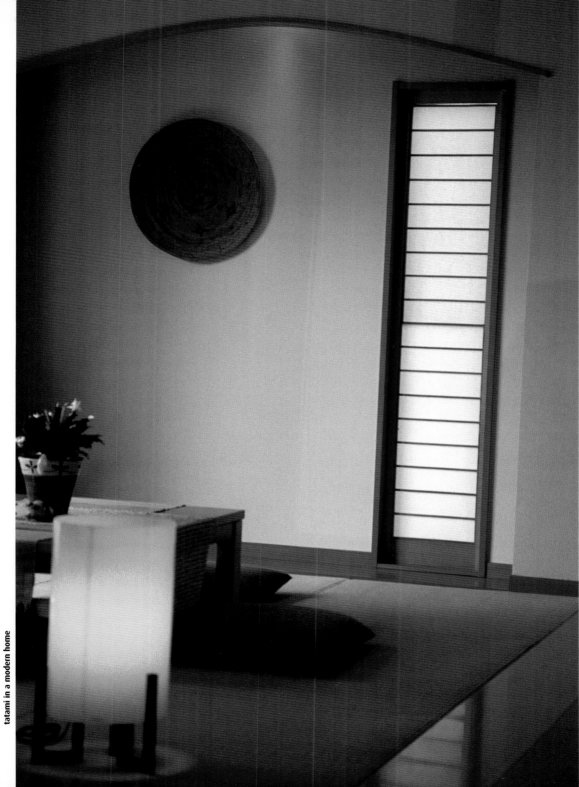

tatami in a modern home

communication & packaging

advertising

homeware

products

73

transport

food & drink

interiors

architecture

fashion

communication & packaging

advertising

homeware

products

74

transport

food & drink

interiors

architecture

fashion

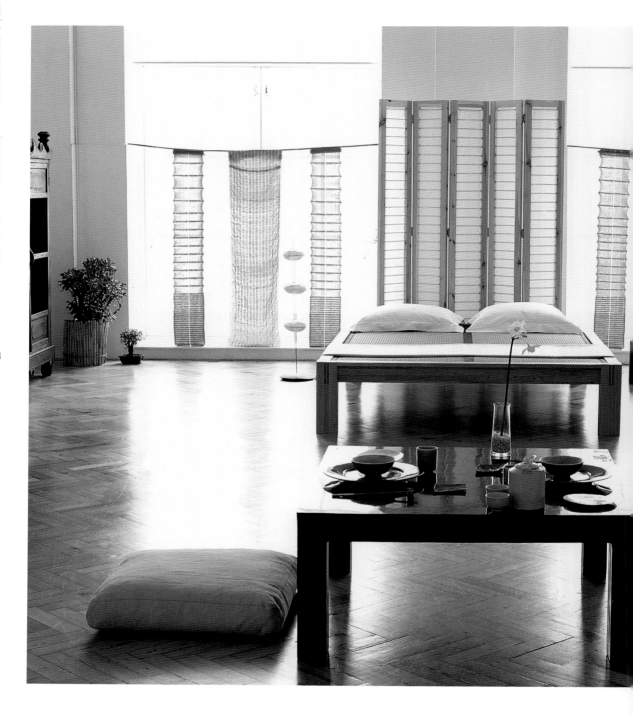

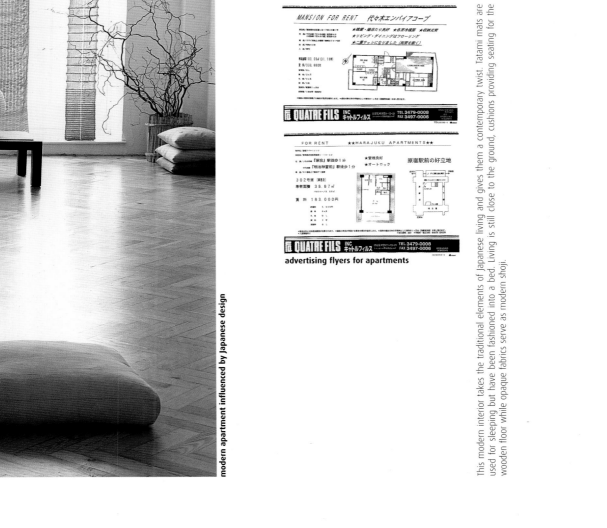

modern apartment influenced by Japanese design

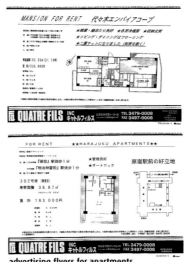

advertising flyers for apartments

This modern interior takes the traditional elements of Japanese living and gives them a contemporary twist. Tatami mats are used for sleeping but have been fashioned into a bed. Living is still close to the ground, cushions providing seating for the wooden floor while opaque fabrics serve as modern shoji.

communication & packaging

advertising

homeware

products

75

transport

food & drink

interiors

architecture

fashion

communication & packaging

advertising

homeware

products

76

transport

food & drink

interiors

architecture

fashion

The layout of the contemporary kitchen has its roots in its traditional counterpart, with a shelf for storing pots and pans and other utensils hung from the wall. A two-ring gas stove is in the corner while a white oven toaster sits upon the fridge.

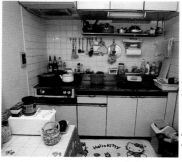

typical Japanese kitchen

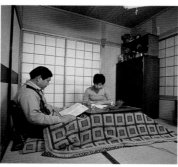

kotatsu

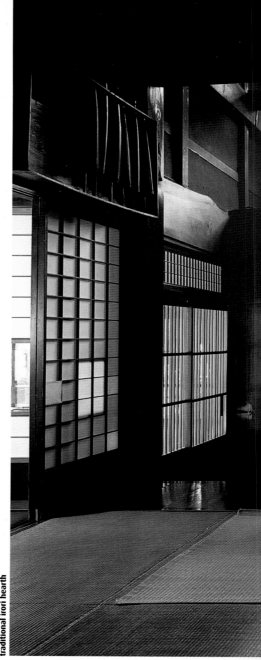

traditional irori hearth

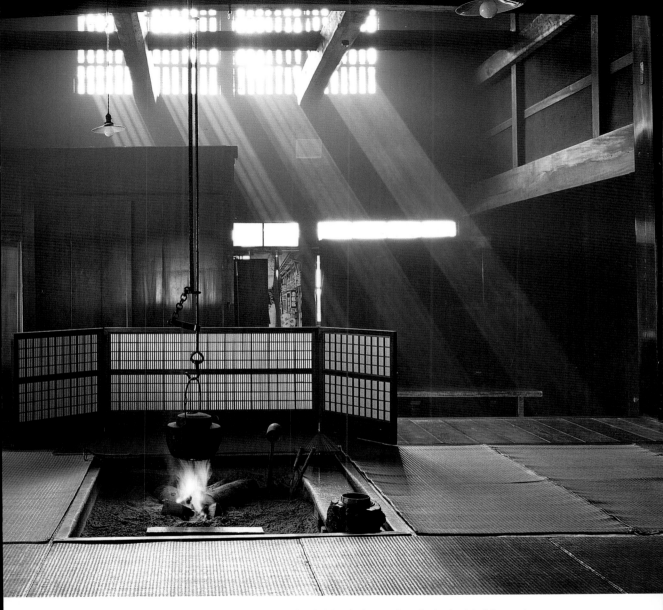

The *kotatsu* (left) is the modern, urban equivalent of the *irori* hearth (above), that was long the focal point of the country household as it was here that meals were eaten and people gathered to keep warm. The kotatsu is a table with a heating element beneath it. A removable top allows a futon-type blanket to be placed underneath providing a cover to trap the heat and keep legs warm.

communication & packaging

advertising

homeware

products

78

transport

food & drink

interiors

architecture

fashion

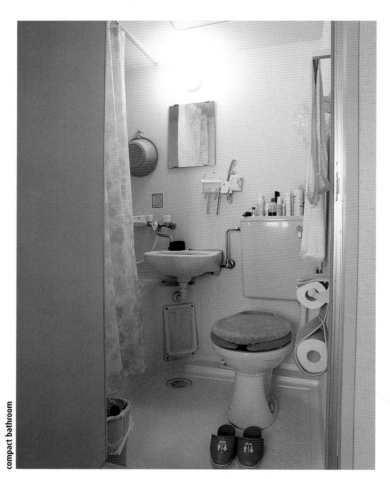

compact bathroom

The unit bathroom shown here is a common fixture in modern apartments. Constructed from one large plastic mould it houses a deep square bath just big enough to sit and soak in, and a shower head, basin and toilet. The Japanese are quite particular about cleanliness and remove their indoor slippers before stepping into their bathroom slippers.

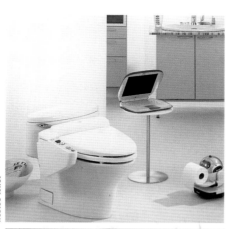

heated toilet

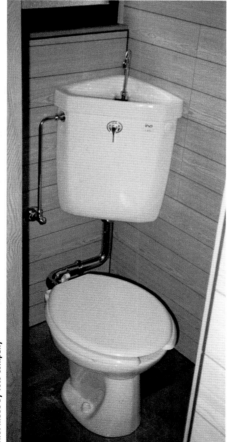

toilet made by Toto Company

The Japanese fascination with toilets highlights both a national penchant for cleanliness and a love of gadgetry. The contemporary Japanese toilet (upper right) now comes with a heated seat and, in lieu of toilet paper, a nozzle that sprays warm water followed by a quick blow dry. The early Western-style toilets in Japan, many of which still exist in older buildings, were designed not only to fill small spaces but were also environmentally friendly as the water used to wash hands was then funnelled into the toilet's water tank. Toilets also came with two types of flush: large and small. While the contemporary wash and blow dry approach to toilets economizes on toilet paper, the etiquette button has been introduced into public bathrooms as a water saving device. Japanese women often flush before using a toilet as it is impolite to be heard. Concern over wastage of water has led to the introduction of the etiquette button, that when pushed gives 15 seconds of the sound of flushing water.

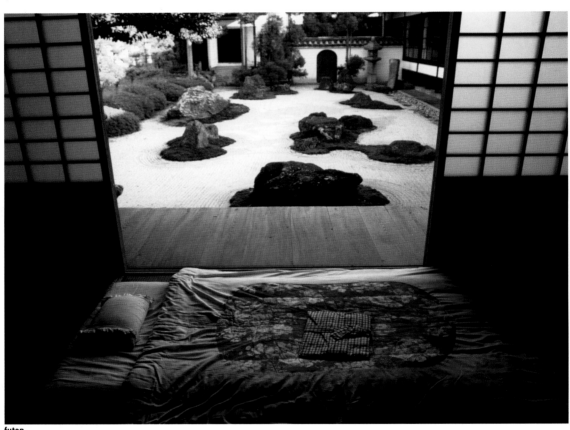

communication & packaging

advertising

homeware

products

80

transport

food & drink

interiors

architecture

fashion

futon

communication & packaging

advertising

homeware

products

81

transport

food & drink

interiors

architecture

fashion

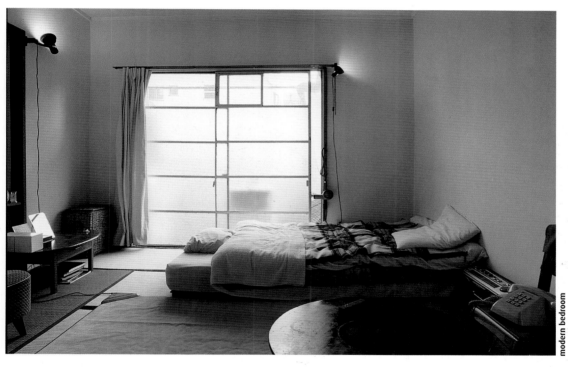

modern bedroom

Although the majority of older people still sleep on futons, the younger generation universally favour beds, usually low ones like the one shown above. Futons come in one size (designed to fit the area of a tatami mat), which means married couples are obliged to sleep separately, hence many prefer a double bed. Once a child is born the mother usually moves into the tatami room and sleeps on a futon with the child for at least the first two years. In some cases where there is very little space, the whole family sleeps on futons in the same room.

communication & packaging

advertising

homeware

products

82

transport

food & drink

interiors

architecture

fashion

Although the Western image of a Japanese home is often one of Zen austerity the reality is quite different. A contemporary lifestyle with televisions, CD players, DVDs and washing machines does not lend itself to the old lifestyle where rooms were multi-functional and furniture could be folded up and put away when not in use. Since old houses and apartments do not have built in wardrobes but rather a large closet where a futon is stored and clothes were at one time folded away flat, many people end up installing large poles across their room, hanging clothes from them or even from the wall. While in the West young people tend to share accommodation, in urban Japan, most tend to live alone in small rooms, thus duplicating the need for every person to own their own fridge, washing machine or television. Lack of space means washing machines are usually kept outside on the balcony and most Japanese use only cold water for their wash. Outdoor slippers are required for the balcony.

interior of Japanese apartment

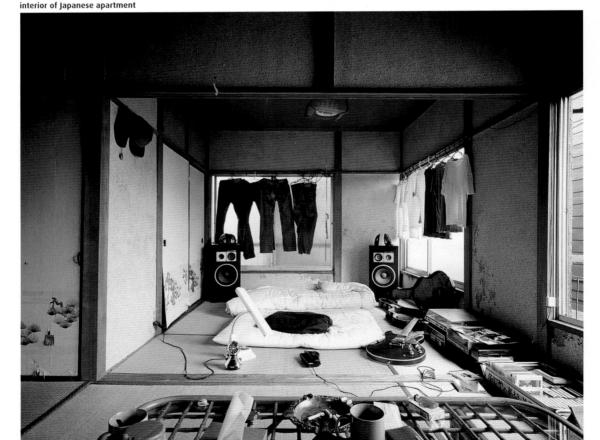

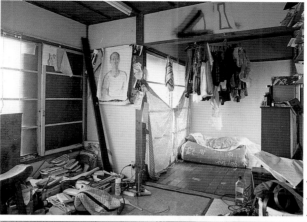

interior of apartment

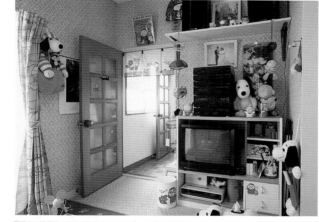

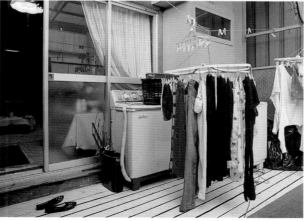

balcony

communication & packaging

advertising

homeware

products

transport

food & drink

interiors

architecture

fashion

84

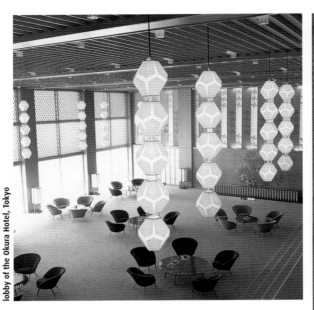

lobby of the Okura Hotel, Tokyo

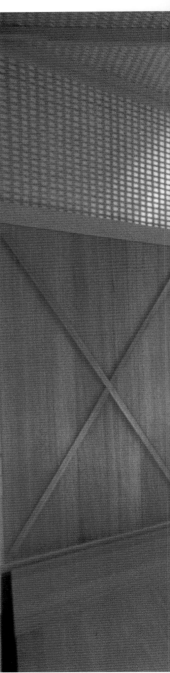

The Okura (above), one of Tokyo's deluxe hotels, offers a glimpse of a Japanese interpretation of 1950s style. Overtones of the American designers Charles and Ray Eames are combined with traditional shoji screens and paper lamps and the lobby still maintains the look of the 1950s, the period when the hotel was constructed.

Shigeru Uchida's contemporary wooden and paper teahouse (right) embodies the four main elements sought in the tea ceremony: harmony, respect, purity and tranquility. Everything in the room from the chaste, seasonal flower display to the tea utensils are specially selected to evoke a certain mood within the space.

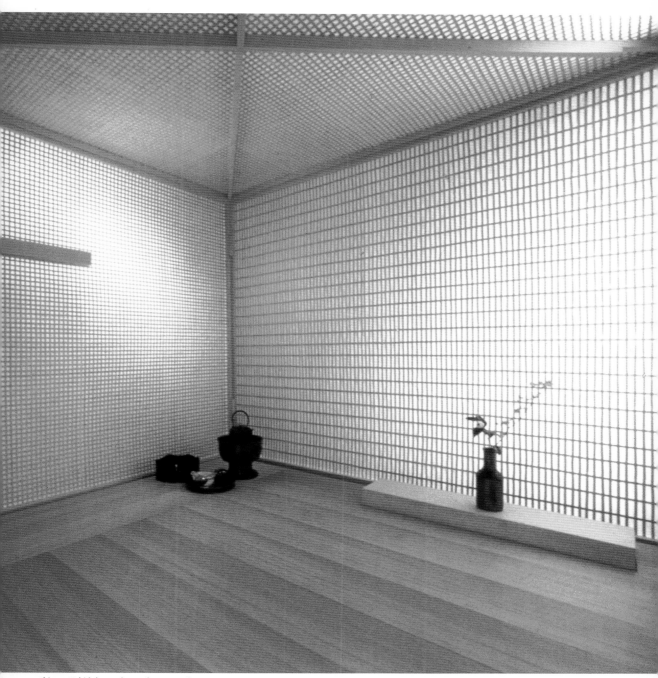

Shigeru Uchida's wooden and paper teahouse

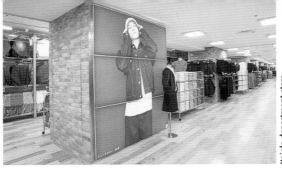

Uniqlo department store

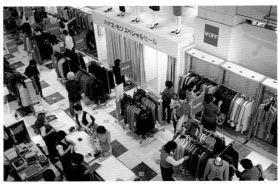

Mastuya department store,

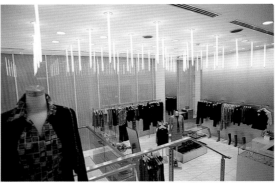

Opaque department store

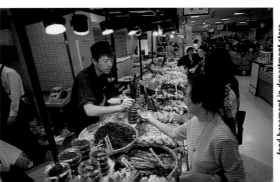

food basement in department store

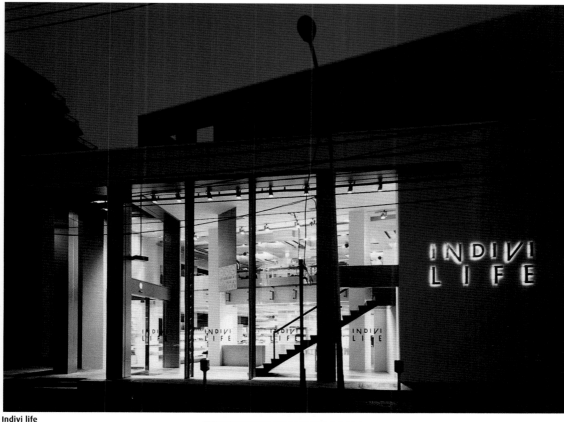

Indivi life

Depato, Japanese department stores, were the initially purveyors of a Western lifestyle, selling clothing, modern household goods and even engagement rings (an alien concept that has been successfully adopted into the culture). While at one time, they educated women on Western-style clothing, ironically they now offer instruction in their own culture such as how to dress in a kimono. Depato have a uniform layout with the clothing sections divided into individual fashion boutiques. The top floor usually has a variety of restaurants while the basement is set up like an old fashioned market.

Department stores had their heyday in the 1980s when their racks overflowed with foreign designer brands. They have since suffered a large decline in sales and have been forced to economize. In their place lifestyle stores, such as Inidivi Life (above) have emerged, selling a variety of select goods ranging from make-up, clothing, homeware to food.

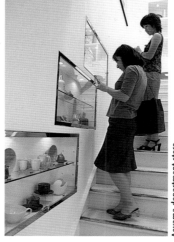

Aoyama department store

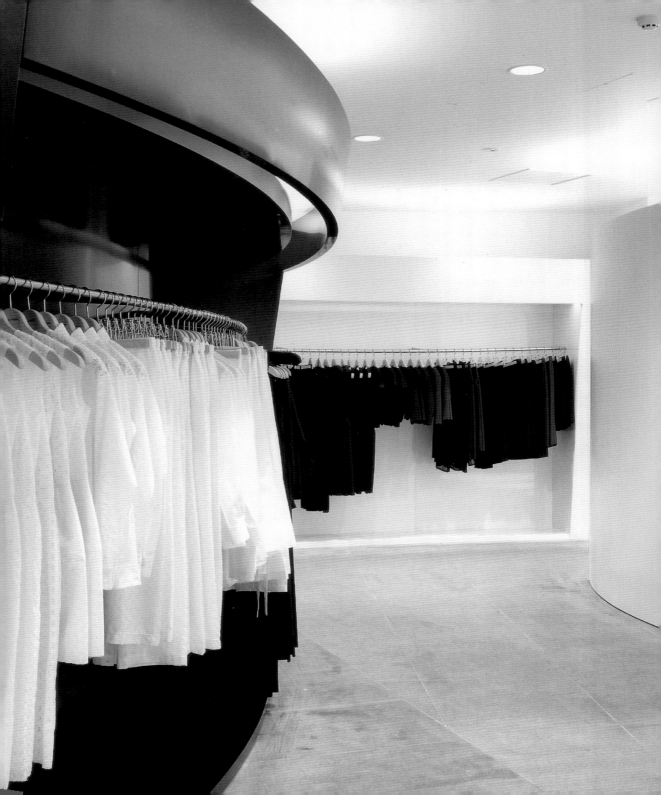

Japanese fashion designers pioneered the white, spare look adopted in store interiors, taking classic elements from traditional Japanese interior design and reinterpreting them into a modernist context. Comme des Garçons' flagship store is a testament to simplicity and restraint. Devoid of superfluous embellishment, clean edges and curved interior walls (some open to the ceiling and others made of glass) create a fluid, open space. Monochromatic colours and basic elements such as wood, stone, glass and concrete provide a subliminal environment for the meticulously displayed goods and clothing.

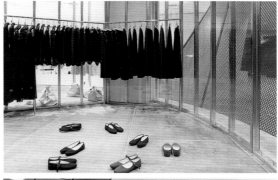

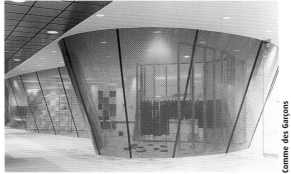

Comme des Garçons

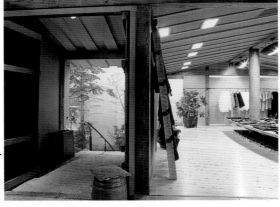

Badou R shop

Badou R, renowned for its line of youth clothing, 45rpm, turned to traditional design for its new store. Located in a residential side street, a stone entrance leads to a wooden house where shoes are removed in exchange for slippers upon entry. Classic materials such as chestnut, cypress and bamboo are incorporated into the building while other traditional materials are given a contemporary twist. Glazed tiles form a subtle design in the wooden floor, indigo *washi* (paper) decorates a screen while tree trunks still bearing bark are embedded with iron hooks for hanging and displaying clothes.

communication & packaging

advertising

homeware

products

90

transport

food & drink

interiors

architecture

fashion

Shintoism has always highlighted the purifying nature of water (hands are washed and mouths rinsed before entering a shrine) and the nightly soak in a bath tub has become an integral part of the Japanese lifestyle. Although the majority of homes today have baths, until comparatively recently people often bathed at the local *sento* – the public bath. Here people scrub down and shower and once clean, soak in the large communal tub. Open from late afternoon to evening, sentos were once at the heart of the neighourhood where people got together at the end of the day, women in one side of the building and men in the other. Although they have been declining in number over the years, sentos are currently enjoying a revival having updated their image with spa treatments, jacuzzi baths and saunas. A visit to a sento or an onsen (hot spring – as shown) is a major form of relaxation in Japan with certain onsen renowned for their ability to cure specific ailments.

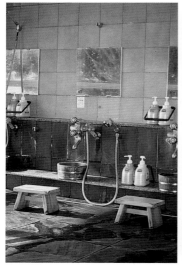

sento

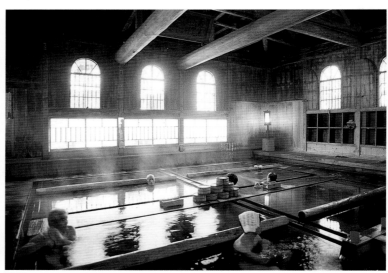

onsen

Capsule hotels are one of Japan's great conveniences. Located near stations and cheaper than a hotel or a taxi ride home, they cater largely to businessmen who fail to catch the last train to the suburbs. Similar to a bunk in a train's sleeper compartment, these self contained units usually have a television, radio and alarm clock at the foot of the bed. Guests can relax in a communal area where there are bathing facilities and clothes are stored in lockers. Accommodation for women exists however the sexes are segregated with capsules for women located in a separate area.

At one time love hotels revelled in the world of fantasy as shown here. Identified by their ornate chateau-like exteriors and names like "Hotel Tiara", rooms were decorated thematically: the Venice room sported a gondola, the jungle room, a Tarzan like interior and the less erotic Edinburgh room had flock wallpaper. A complimentary pack of condoms and box of tissues were standard fare. These days, particularly in urban areas, love hotels tend to be more subdued affairs with interiors resembling fashionable boutique hotels. Many young people use them not just for love trysts but as a means to escape and party with friends or as a place to relax and spend the night singing karaoke. Rooms are rented by the night or in two hour sessions during the day.

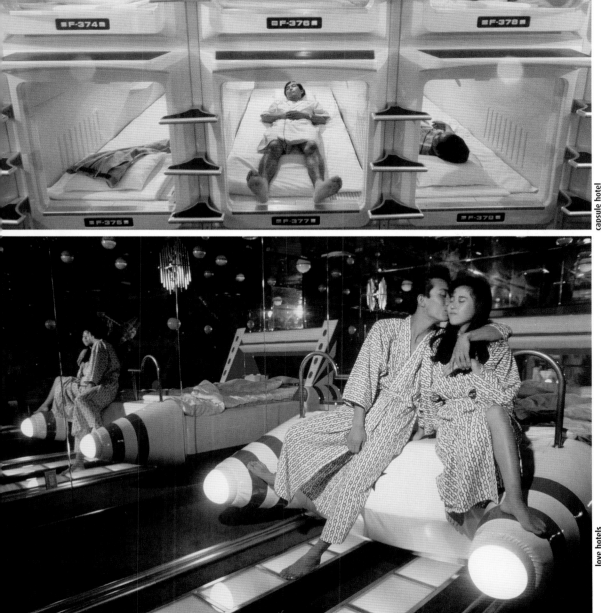

F-374 F-376 F-378

F-375 F-377 F-379

love hotels

food & drink

communication & packaging

advertising

homeware

products

92

transport

food & drink

interiors

architecture

fashion

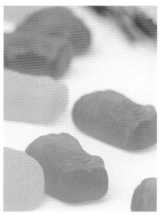

Japan has one of the healthiest diets in the world, envied just as much for its low fat content as it is for its exquisite presentation. When Buddhism was introduced from China in the Sixth Century, the Japanese renounced meat in favour of a primarily vegetarian diet. It was not until 1868, after over 200 years of self imposed isolation that Japan opened its doors to the outside world and meat was slowly reintroduced to the general population.

Most of Japan's land is mountainous and difficult to cultivate so natural resources are heavily relied upon including roots and vegetables from the mountains and fish and seaweed from the ocean. Rice is the quintessential food of Japan, offered daily at the family altar and used in Buddhist funeral ceremonies. The Japanese word for rice is *gohan* which also means meal. It is the principle ingredient of *sake* – rice wine – which is also the general word for alcohol and the ceremonial drink at Shinto weddings. These days despite a cosmopolitan diet, rice is still served daily in most homes.

A traditional, formal Japanese meal consists of a series of small dishes served in a prescribed order. Beginning with *sashimi* (raw fish), a clear soup and seasonal appetizers, dishes containing meat, tofu, fish and vegetables that are grilled, simmered or fried follow. Each dish is prepared differently so the cooking method is not duplicated. Although spicy flavours such as *wasabi* (Japanese horseradish), radish and ginger are added on the side, the key to cooking is to preserve or heighten the natural flavours of the food. As a final course, rice, pickles, green tea and sometimes miso soup are served. The only thing that changes is the quantity of dishes served, otherwise the same order is followed whether the meal be a simple fish dish at home or a twelve-course *kaiseki* meal, Japan's equivalent of *haute-cuisine*.

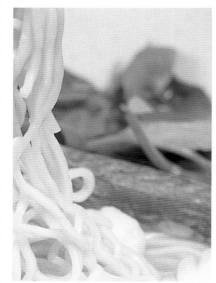

Beyond format, an equally essential aspect of Japanese cuisine is presentation. The visual appeal of a meal is intrinsically tied to taste. Taste is quickly diminished if there is no thought put into appearance. Plates and bowls are chosen to best show off the food with both colour and shape taken into consideration, square food complemented by round dishes and vice versa. Integrated into this sensibility is a heightened appreciation of the seasons, reflected both in the choice of food and style of presentation. Seasonal ingredients such as bamboo sprouts and bonito fish are used in the spring, boiled *edamame* (soya beans) and eel in the summer and pumpkin and mushrooms in autumn. Small additional garnishes such as cherry blossom petals floating in a clear soup or carrots carved into maple leaves further enhance the seasonal imagery.

Many dishes are actually eaten according to the season. Hot thick noodles and *nabe* (stews) appear on menus in winter, while eel is eaten to provide stamina in the long, humid summers. Despite the advent of air conditioning, blocks of tofu served over ice and *somen,* vermicelli-size noodles floating in cold water in a hollowed half of a bamboo trunk, are classic summer dishes that provide mental relief from the stifling heat, even if they are no longer a physical necessity.

Japan is quite the gourmet culture and offers more variety of world cuisines than any other country: Italian, French and Asian food all enjoy enormous popularity. There are a multitude of cooking magazines and television gourmet shows, the latter often featuring an intrepid reporter scouring the corners of Japan in pursuit of a special regional dish. The Japanese love to eat and eating out is an integral part of life as limited space means entertaining usually happens outside the home. Unlike the West where eating out is sometimes marked by a sense of occasion, Japanese dining provides a sense of community. Office workers at the end of the day will often gather in an *izakaya* (a small bar serving food) with colleagues and enjoy a beer and sake accompanied by small dishes of food placed in the middle of the table and shared by all. The food is picked at slowly and more dishes are added as the evening proceeds. Young urbanites, many of whom live

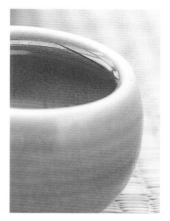

alone in small apartments, will either pick up something at their local convenience store on the way home or just as easily drop by the neighbourhood ramen shop for a bowl of noodles, in the same way that someone in the West would drop by a pub or a café. There is no stigma attached to dining alone and the layout of most Japanese restaurants, with a long counter and groups of tables,

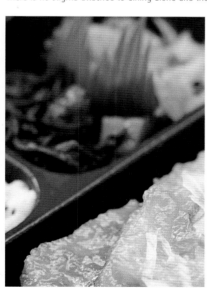

makes it easy to accommodate both single diners and large groups of people. Many local restaurants provide magazines and have televisions so the restaurant doubles as a home.

Japanese restaurants tend to be small family run businesses with the husband cooking and the wife serving. The chef is universally referred to as "master" having earned the position through years of apprenticeship under another master. Unlike the West where the chef is often out of sight in a kitchen, the master is on full view. There is an element of entertainment in Japanese cuisine as the chef slices fish, grills vegetables or prepares a bowl of noodles, right in front of the diner.

Sashimi sliced from a fish taken fresh from a tank then presented with the twitching fish carcass or live "dancing" prawns dipped in boiling oil then eaten, attest to this. Even the ubiquitous bento box is designed to delight. While the clear plastic tops of the cheaper bentos reveal their contents, the more expensive lacquer bento box remains a surprise until opened, when it will be studied copiously, admired, then consumed. Presentation is not limited to lacquerware, even something as mundane as the *hinomaru* bento, a plastic box of rice with a red *umeboshi* (sour plum) planted in the middle, transforms a bland white image into a national symbol.

communication & packaging

advertising

homeware

products

94

transport

food & drink

interiors

architecture

fashion

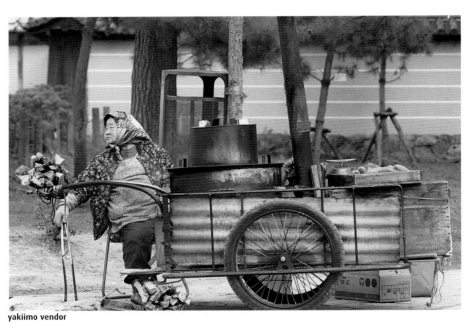

yakiimo vendor

Street vendors have long been an integral part of Japanese life with their unique shouts and cries. In Edo times, peddlers were a common sight selling fish and vegetables, everyday household items and medicines, while not so long ago it was still possible to buy fresh tofu from hand pushed carts announced by a bell or whistle. Although street vendors are slowly disappearing, the *yakiimo* (sweet potato) seller still remains. Yakiimo are baked in a wood-fired stove and are sold during the chilly winter months. Even though the wooden handcart is slowly being replaced by trucks and the wail of "yakiimo", substituted with an automated tape, yakiimo vendors are still an important fixture in the urban landscape.

communication & packaging

advertising

homeware

products

transport

95

food & drink

architecture

interiors

fashion

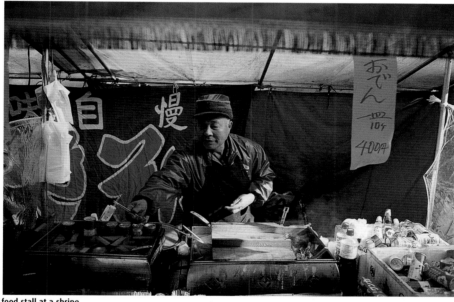

food stall at a shrine

Oden, like yakiimo, makes its appearance in autumn. The dish is a combination of fish paste dumplings, fried tofu, eggs, and vegetables such as *konyaku* and *daikon* (Japanese radish) cooked in a broth. Accompanied by mustard and eaten like a stew, oden is often found at stalls on the side of the street. *Tako yaki*, (octopus balls in a dough like batter, as shown overleaf), grilled corn on the cob, and fish-shaped cakes filled with sweet bean paste are other foods that are commonly sold on the street. Over the years, oden has also become a staple of 24-hour convenience stores known as *konbini*, and the strong smell of the broth permeates the stores during the winter months.

communication & packaging

advertising

homeware

products

96

transport

food & drink

interiors

architecture

fashion

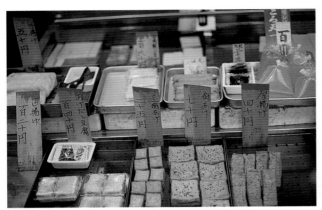

tofu shop, Osaka

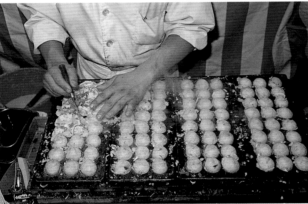

tako yaki – octopus balls

Ramen is not only an early form of fast food, it is also one of Japan's most popular foods. Chinese in origin, ramen noodles are made from flour and are often eaten standing up at counters in shops, and sometimes at stands on railway station platforms. The Japanese can become quite passionate over the issue of ramen – there is a museum devoted to the topic – and nothing divides them more than an allegiance for a regional broth: Hakata in Kyushu is renowned for its pork-based broth, while Sapporo in the North uses a miso-based soup. Although ramen can be served cold in summer, it is typically served piping hot with a selection of toppings such as sliced pork, seaweed, bamboo shoots and a slice of pink and white fishcake.

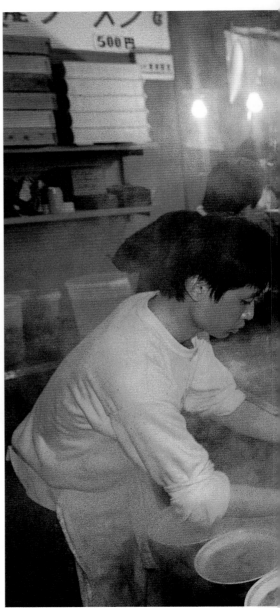

ramen shop in Osaka

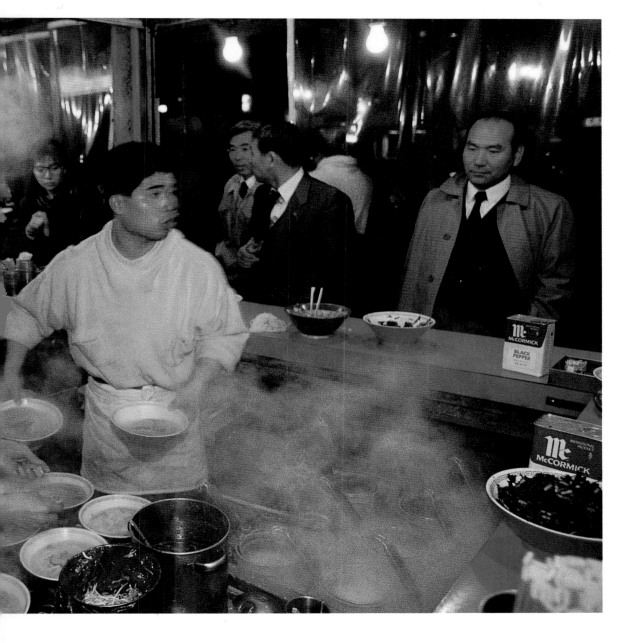

communication & packaging

advertising

homeware

products

97

transport

food & drink

interiors

architecture

fashion

communication & packaging

advertising

homeware

products

98

transport

food & drink

interiors

architecture

fashion

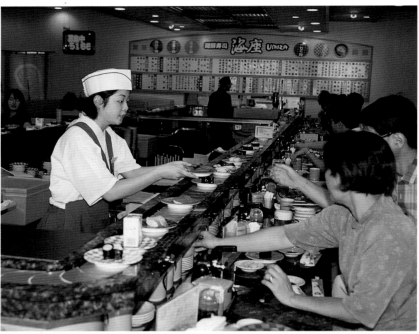
rotating sushi counter

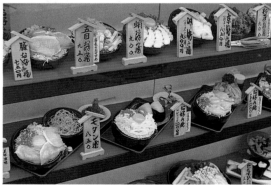
plastic food menu

Japanese food relies on its inherent natural flavour, which is why fish is often eaten raw. In a typical sushi bar, a glass case shows the selection of fish available. The sushi chef slices the fish according to order then adds a dash of wasabi, moulding it to the rice, which is then served on a wooden board accompanied by pickled ginger. It is quite common for a customer to defer to the sushi master, relying on his expertise to select the fish. Comparatively speaking, sushi is seen as a luxury food in Japan. Rotating sushi on the other hand has long been viewed as the poor man's sushi. Pre-made sushi (and therefore not as fresh) is served on small plastic plates that rotate on a conveyor belt around the counter of a restaurant. Customers select their sushi as it passes by and the bill is totalled according to the number of empty plates left. Recently there has been a trend to upgrade the image of the latter with the opening of more fashionable restaurants featuring rotating sushi, in part influenced by the success of such establishments overseas. While rotating sushi allows the customer a view of what is to be served, many Japanese restaurants rely on plastic displays outside which serve as a visual menu.

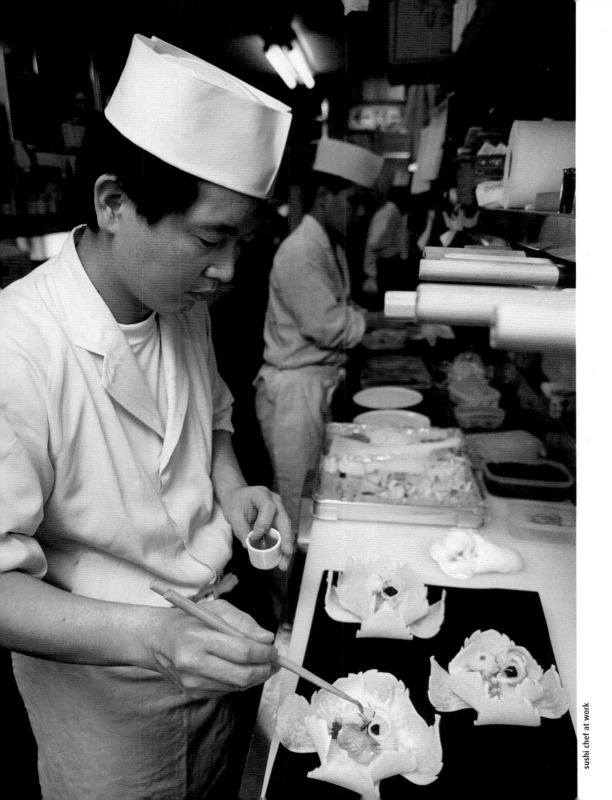

99

sushi chef at work

communication & packaging

advertising

homeware

products

100

transport

food & drink

interiors

architecture

fashion

Noodles are an integral part of Japanese culture, their long, thin shape symbolizing longevity. Presented to new neighbours as a token of friendship, they are also eaten on New Year's Eve to ensure a year of good health. At one time they were customarily eaten before departing on a long journey to guarantee a safe return, which is why so many noodle shops were established near railway stations. Long a staple of the Japanese diet, noodles come in a variety of forms. *Soba* noodles are made from buckwheat ground into flour and are beige in colour although green tea may also be added to colour them. *Udon* are larger than soba and are either flat or round and are made from wheat flour. *Somen* noodles are also made from wheat but are very fine.

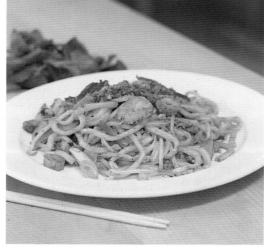

udon noodles

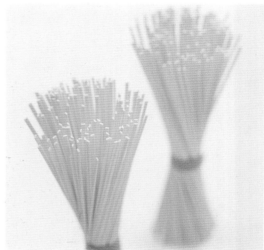

dried noodles

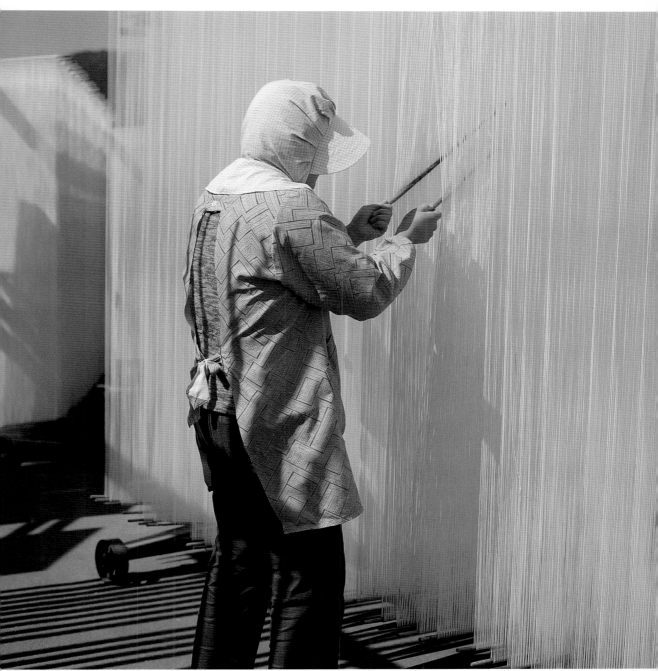

making somen noodles

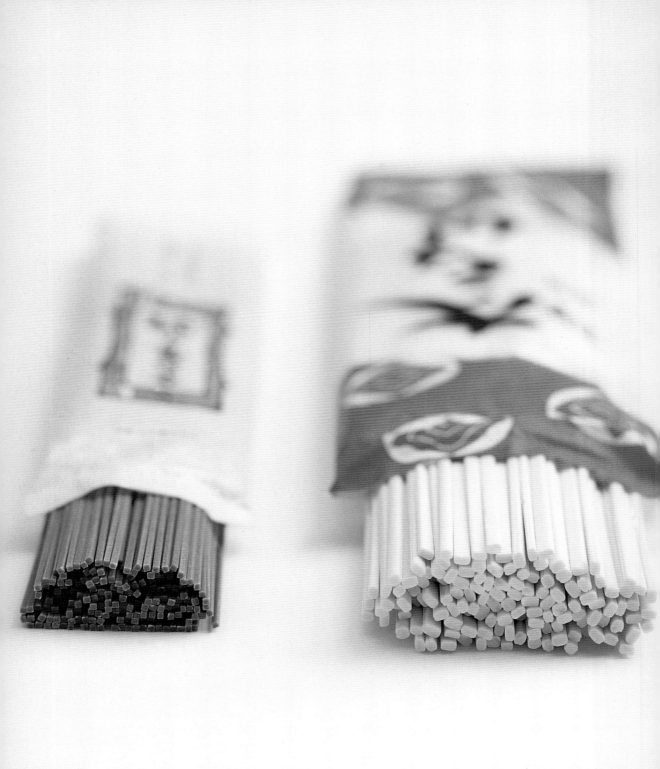

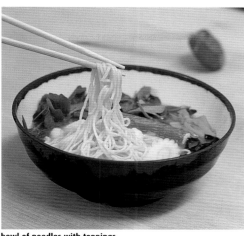

bowl of noodles with toppings

Most noodles come dried in packets although the tastiest are those that are freshly made. The best restaurants make their noodles by hand on the premises. Like ramen, soba and udon can be accompanied by a variety of toppings, such as tempura fried shrimp, mountain vegetables or deep fried tofu. Udon noodles are also popular with curry sauce. Noodles are usually served in a piping hot broth, etiquette requires that they are slurped so the noodles are consumed as quickly as possible to prevent them from softening in the liquid. Instant noodles are immensely popular because of their low cost, although when they were first introduced in the 1950s they were perceived as a luxury item. More expensive than the handmade noodles that were widely available at the time, instant ramen became an exclusive item. Nowadays the situation is completely reversed.

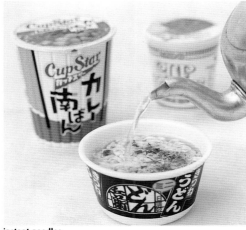

instant noodles

communication & packaging

advertising

homeware

products

103

transport

food & drink

interiors

architecture

fashion

communication & packaging

advertising

homeware

products

104

transport

food & drink

interiors

architecture

fashion

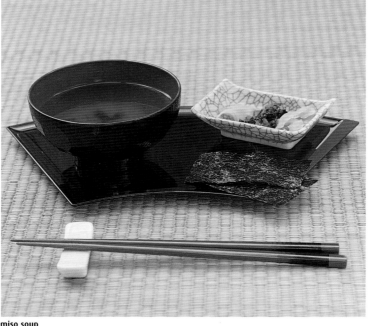

miso soup

Like noodles, soup is an intrinsic part of the Japanese diet. Traditionally it was served for breakfast but today's younger generation tends towards a more Western-style breakfast of bread and coffee. Nevertheless, *miso shiru* still accompanies rice at the end of a meal. The key ingredient to a good soup lies in the *dashi* (stock), which is made from flakes of dried bonito fish and kelp. Although instant dashi is widely available, it bears no comparison to the traditional version. Packed with protein, miso is a fermented soya bean paste sold in plastic tubs. There are various types of miso some with wheat and barley added, the two most distinct ones are yellow miso, which is somewhat sweet, and red miso, which is darker and more savoury in flavour. Miso is not confined to soups and is frequently used as a dressing or topping for vegetables.

communication & packaging

advertising

homeware

products

105

transport

food & drink

interiors

architecture

fashion

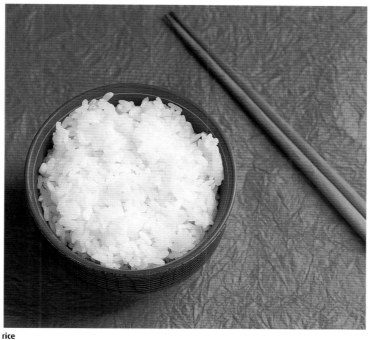

rice

No other food is tied to Japan's national identity in the way that rice is. It is symbolically offered to the Gods, and there is a goddess of rice whose messenger, the fox, guards the entrance to shrines across the country. Consumed since the third century, rice by-products have long been incorporated into the Japanese lifestyle, and have been used to make clothing, footwear, paper and housing. Rice is an essential aspect of the Japanese diet with a short-grain, glutinous variety favoured. Unlike other dishes that are served in individual portions ahead of time, rice is served at the table from a large lidded bowl, although in most homes today the latter has been replaced by an electric rice cooker. Although *gohan* is the Japanese word for rice, when served as part of a Western dish, such as curry rice, it is referred to by its Western name, *rai-su*.

communication & packaging

advertising

homeware

products

106

transport

food & drink

interiors

architecture

fashion

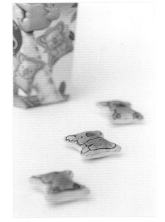

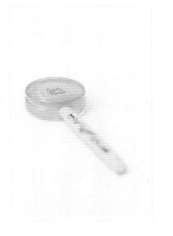

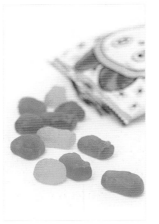

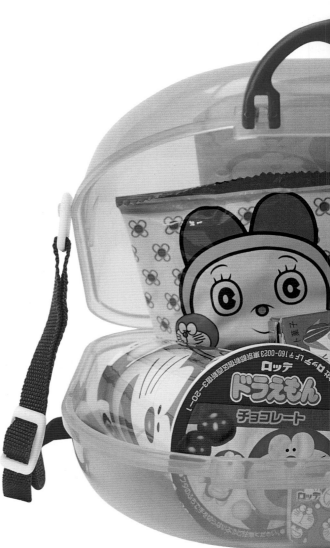

communication & packaging

advertising

homeware

products

107

transport

food & drink

interiors

architecture

fashion

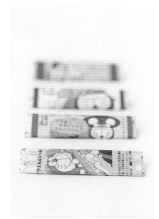

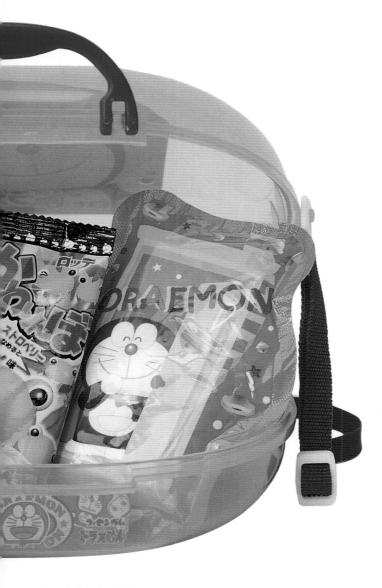

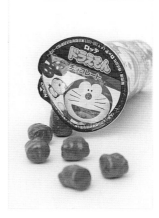

character-based confectionery

The market for children's sweets in Japan is dominated by character goods, including the extremely popular "Hello Kitty", "Doraemon" and "Pokémon". Cuteness dominates and sweets come in vibrant colourful packaging with names like *Peko Poko Choco*, *Momo no Fooa* and *Melty Kiss*. While Western flavours such as strawberry cheesecake and café latte are popular, Japanese flavours are frequently used, for example green tea chocolate and bubble gum in ginseng and plum flavours. Japan's love for the miniature is evinced in the detail of decoration: minute Doraemon chocolate figures, miniature biscuits sandwiched with chocolate to resemble tiny burgers, and a child-size cup of instant noodles full of sweets moulded into noodle shapes.

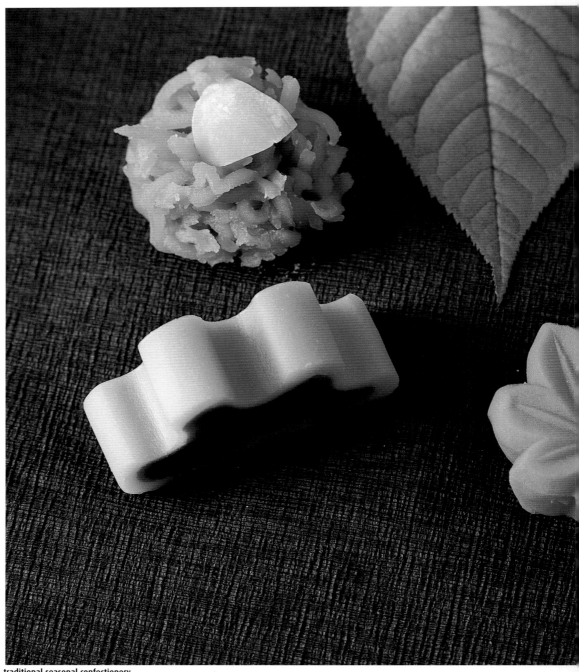

communication & packaging

advertising

homeware

products

108

transport

food & drink

interiors

architecture

fashion

traditional seasonal confectionery

Wagashi are the exquisite, traditional handmade Japanese confections that were created to accompany the tea ceremony, their sweetness designed to offset the bitter taste of green tea. Intricate in design, the colour and shapes of the sweets reflect the different seasons. Cherry-pink rice cakes wrapped in a *sakura* (cherry) leaf appear in spring, while maple leaves and seasonal colours announce the arrival of autumn as shown here.

communication & packaging

advertising

homeware

products

110

transport

food & drink

interiors

architecture

fashion

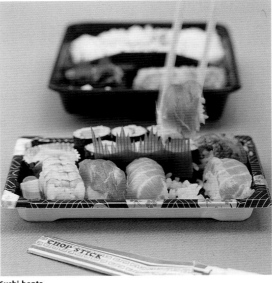

Sushi bento

Bento (Japanese lunch boxes) are the mainstay of Japanese cuisine, served at corporate lunches, eaten under the trees at cherry blossom viewing parties and carried to school by children for lunch. A typical bento usually contains a little bit of everything: rice, fish, meat, vegetables and pickles. The more expensive *kaiseki* lunchbox reflects the seasons in its wide range of ingredients while a love of the visual is manifest in the choice of colours and delicate presentation of the food. Bentos range from magnificent lacquered boxes served in fine restaurants to the ubiquitous clear top plastic boxes sold at 24-hour convenience stores. Homemade lunch boxes for children often contain rice moulded into animal shapes, or decorated in the image of a panda's face. *Kiben* are lunch boxes sold at railway stations throughout the country and are renowned for their regional ingredients.

The Japanese delight in regional foods and a trip to the country is invariably accompanied by the purchase of local produce known as *meibutsu* which can range from pickles and wasabi to butter cookies.

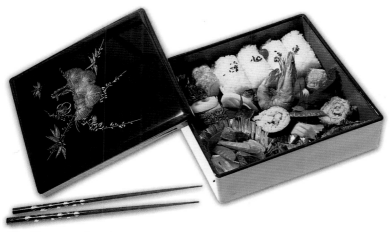

traditional lacquerware bento box

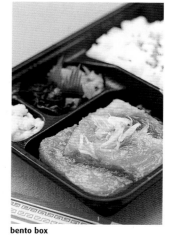

bento box

communication & packaging

advertising

homeware

products

transport

111

food & drink

interiors

architecture

fashion

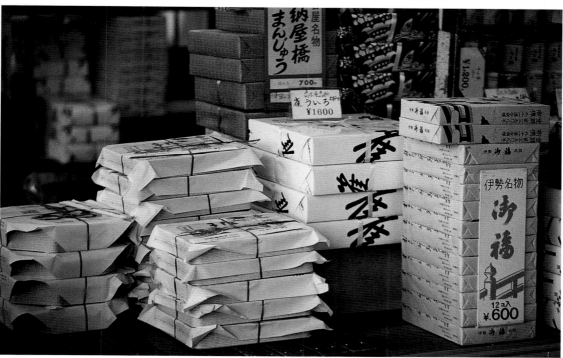

meibutsu

112

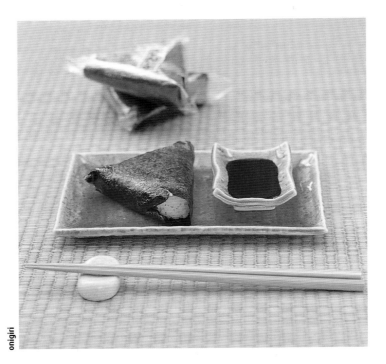

onigiri

Onigiri, balls of rice wrapped in seaweed, are the Japanese equivalent of sandwiches. A basic item in the homemade lunchbox, they are a practical way to use leftover rice and fillings vary from pickled plum to salmon. Onigiri are also one of the most popular items at convenience stores although when they were first introduced they did not sell well. Sellers responded by coming up with more creative fillings that are now standard onigiri fare such as the highly popular tuna mayonnaise. Onigiri may also be ordered in *izakaya* where they come grilled with a crispy soy sauce coating.

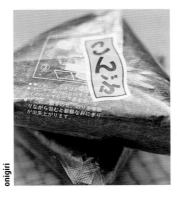

onigiri

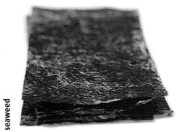

seaweed

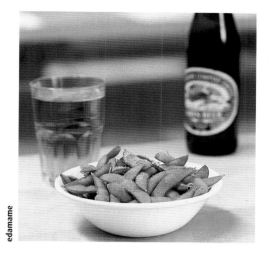

edamame

Edamame – green soya beans eaten from their pods – are typically found during the summer months. Boiled in slightly salted water they are packed with protein and are usually served as an appetizer to accompany beer.

Gyoza are Chinese dumplings stuffed with a meat or vegetable filling and are frequently served with a bowl of ramen. The Japanese like to nibble at food while they drink, especially at izakaya and often order a variety of small dishes of food throughout the evening.

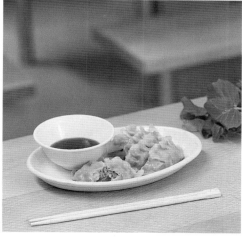

gyoza

communication & packaging

advertising

homeware

products

113

transport

food & drink

interiors

architecture

fashion

communication & packaging

advertising

homeware

products

114

transport

food & drink

interiors

architecture

fashion

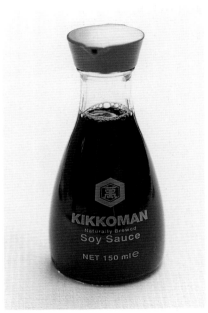

soy sauce

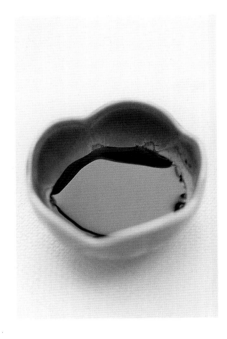

communication & packaging

advertising

homeware

products

transport

food & drink

interiors

architecture

fashion

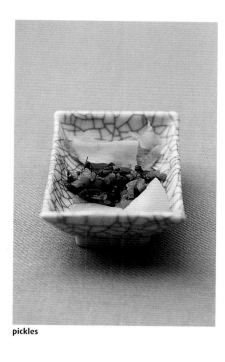

pickles

Soy sauce is one of the mainstays of Japanese cuisine, frequently used as an ingredient in cooking as well as a dipping sauce for dishes such as sushi and tempura. It was introduced to Japan from China in the sixth century and is used throughout Asia. Kikkoman, the company renowned for its famous red-capped bottle, has been producing soy sauce since the seventeenth century and still uses a natural fermentation process in its production process.

Before the days of refrigeration, Japanese preserved their food through drying, smoking and pickling. Until recently it was common for most families to have a large barrel of pickles stored in the home that was used daily. Today a meal ends with a bowl of rice, pickles and a bowl of miso soup, however, in more frugal times, rice and pickles were seen as a complete meal. Each region has its own speciality pickle but typical vegetables for pickling include daikon, eggplant, cucumber and plums.

115

communication & packaging

advertising

homeware

products

116

transport

food & drink

interiors

architecture

fashion

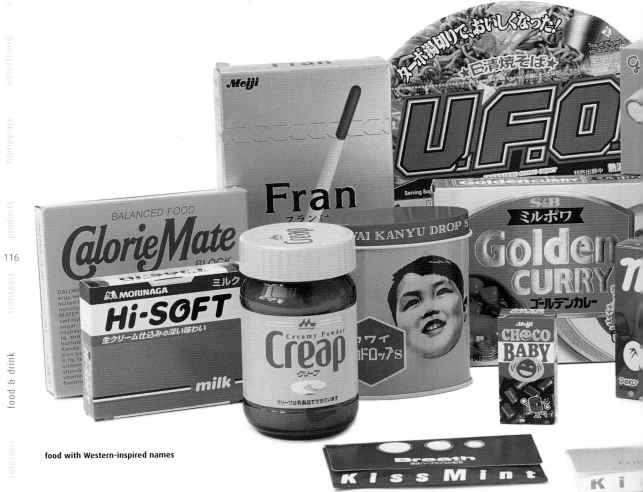

food with Western-inspired names

communication & packaging
advertising
homeware
products
117
transport
food & drink
interiors
architecture
fashion

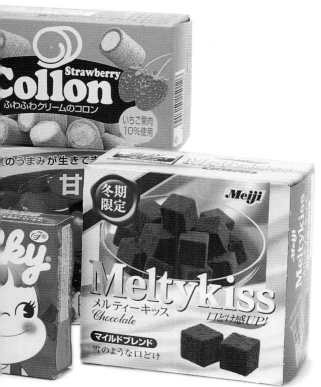

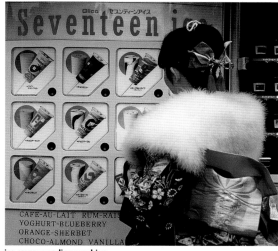

ice cream vending machine

CAFE-AU-LAIT RUM-RAIS
YOGHURT-BLUEBERRY
ORANGE-SHERBET
CHOCO-ALMOND VANILLA

The Japanese often resort to innovative English in the naming of their food products. The milk substitute *Creap* and the sweet *Milky* have been around for years while *Melty Kiss* and *Speed* (a sports drink) are newcomers. *Fran* is a sophisticated rival version of a highly popular snack stick called *Pocky*, which comes in several flavours including savoury, chocolate and strawberry as well as the recently released *Men's Pocky*. Innovation is not solely confined to names: stamina drinks are now being marketed to children, while a new bubble gum is being touted for its ability to cure hangovers.

communication & packaging

advertising

homeware

products

118

transport

food & drink

interiors

architecture

fashion

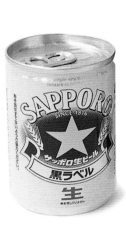
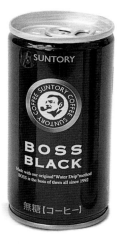
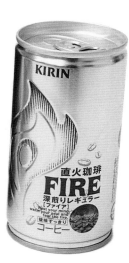

miniature beer and coffee cans

Miniature cans of drinks fill Japan's vending machines, some only sipping size, as with the drinks shown here. A row of cans in one machine may be devoted to the same type of coffee with only slight variations: hot, cold, mild or strong. Japan first began selling coffee in *kissaten* (coffee shops) over one hundred years ago. Kissaten charged a premium for coffee but customers could stay as long as they wanted and enjoy the newspapers, magazines provided while listening the latest jazz. Each cup of coffee was individually brewed with a precision usually reserved for the tea ceremony. Today the homely kissaten are slowly being replaced with chains such as Doutor and Starbucks, whose cheaper prices and Italian-style coffee appeal to the youth market.

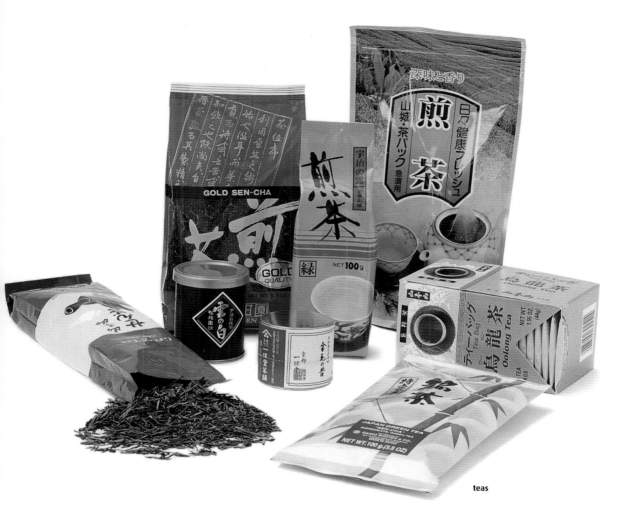

communication & packaging

advertising

homeware

products

119

transport

food & drink

interiors

architecture

fashion

teas

Traditional Japanese tea is green and is a ubiquitous brew drunk throughout the country. Served as a complimentary drink in Japanese restaurants, it is also given to visitors in offices and homes. The type of green tea served depends upon the formality of the occasion. While guests in a domestic environment may be served the more superior *sencha*, lower grade leaf tea, *bancha*, is served in restaurants. The most refined tea is *matcha*, and is used in *chanoyu*, the traditional tea ceremony. Made from dried tea leaves that are crushed into a powder, matcha is whisked into a green frothy, unique bitter brew.

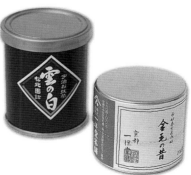

communication & packaging

advertising

homeware

products

120

transport

food & drink

interiors

architecture

fashion

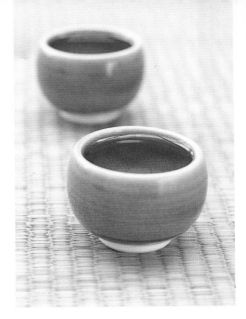

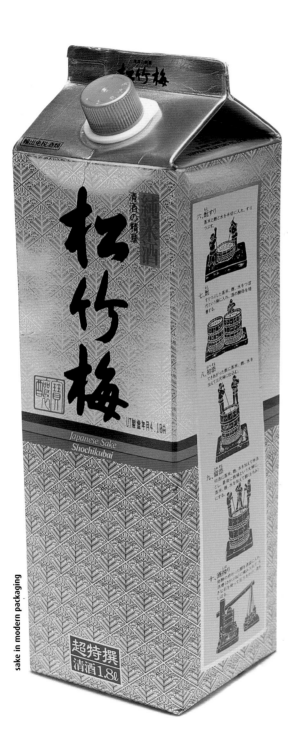

sake in modern packaging

Just as good wine requires quality grapes, good sake requires quality rice. Sake is made from a combination of rice, water and *koji*, the latter being a mould that induces the fermentation process. Water quality is equally important and spring water is preferred. While wine may improve with age, sake should be drunk within a year. There are thousands of different sakes produced in Japan, each labelled to indicate its age, the brewery where it was produced and the alcoholic content. Sake is best served chilled, although it can be a pleasant accompaniment to a meal when served at room temperature. Serving sake is one of Japan's communal rituals and to serve oneself is considered bad manners. Elders and superiors are served first, while it is polite for those receiving sake to hold up their cup and then to take a sip before putting the cup down.

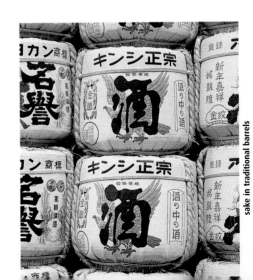

sake in traditional barrels

communication & packaging

advertising

homeware

products

transport

121

food & drink

interiors

architecture

fashion

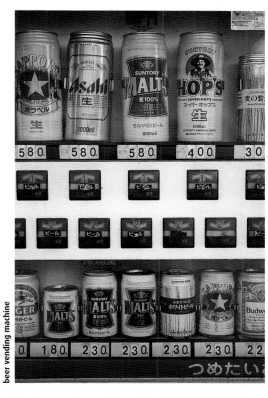

beer vending machine

Beer, known as *bee-ru*, is the most popular alcoholic drink in Japan and has been around since it was first introduced in the Meiji period when people began drinking German and British beer. The latter proved too bitter for the Japanese and German-style beer became the standard. There are four major breweries in Japan all of which produce a similar range of beers from All-Malt to Super-Dry. It is quite common to drink beer before having sake especially in a group. Beer is sold in most drinking establishments although Japan has its own beer halls and in summer, beer gardens open on the roofs of department stores. One of the most convenient ways to purchase beer is from the numerous vending machines that line the side of the road dispensing liquor between the hours of five in the morning and eleven at night.

transport

Renowned for its efficient, speedy and reliable train service, travel in Japan is best symbolized by the _Shinkansen_, familiarly known as the "bullet train", which runs the length of the country – no mean feat given the harsh mountainous topography of the archipelago. In comparison narrow roads, too many cars and congested highways make car travel a less attractive alternative. Domestic air travel has traditionally been more expensive than rail but is becoming increasingly competitive in an effort to encourage customer growth; the continued upgrading of trains and speedier services has, however, enabled rail travel to maintain its popularity.

The Shinkansen made its debut in 1964, the year of the Japanese Olympics with a service between Tokyo and Osaka. Since then the Japanese have been in an ongoing battle with the French and their TGV for title of the world's fastest train. The original blue and white bullet train has been steadily replaced over the years by sleeker, more aerodynamic models. The latest 700 Nozomi series has reduced the ride between Tokyo and Hakata, a distance of over 900 kilometres (600 miles), to just under five hours at a maximum speed of 300 kilometres (185 miles) per hour. Railways are the arteries of Japan, so where the Shinkansen terminates, local trains chug off into more remote corners. Conversely, the myriad of railway lines that fan out into the suburbs converge upon Japan's major city centres, linking them to a network of subway lines, which is by far the easiest way to travel. At rush hour, trains may run as frequently as every two minutes. Only on the rare occasion that there is a delay, when a train or subway platform overflows with crowds, does it become apparent how remarkably efficient the system actually is. The concept of personal space takes on a new meaning when commuters are crammed into carriages cheek by jowl at rush hour, even more uncomfortable in the humid months of summer. What appears as good manners is in fact a form of survival as passengers queue neatly behind marked lines on the platform awaiting the arrival of the next train; once the doors open, people spill out en masse and the crowd gravitates towards the nearest exits, lines of automated ticket machines expediting the process. The efficiency and extensive network of mass transit makes owning a car somewhat redundant in major urban areas.

Despite this, most families place a high priority on car ownership even

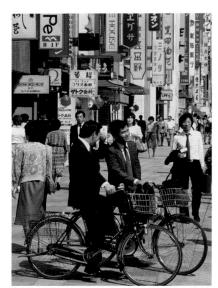

though for many, use will likely be confined to weekends and a couple of annual trips to visit relatives in the country. As a rule, cars are kept in immaculate condition, white being the popular and safe, uniform colour of choice. Japan's rigorous _shaken_, mandatory check ups, ensure that cars are kept in full working order and comply to a strict set of maintenance rules. Shaken is not cheap and is one of the major expenses of car ownership. It is ironic that a country renowned for

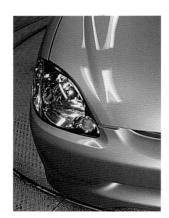

communication & packaging

advertising

homeware

products

123

transport

food & drink

interiors

architecture

fashion

its car production should actually have so little space to accommodate them, particularly in towns and cities. To own a car in Japan first requires proof of parking. Garages are considered a luxury and parking spaces are expensive. New homes on a limited plot will carve out just enough space on the ground floor for a car to be parked. To navigate Japan's narrow, winding roads, especially in the country, numerous curved mirrors on poles are deployed to enable drivers to see round corners as it is often impossible for two cars to pass.

The perpetual redesigning and refining of cars by Japanese manufacturers, to make them more compact and versatile is ongoing. Manufacturers have addressed this dilemma with a sub category of cars referred to as *kei-sha*. These are "lightweight" cars, otherwise known as mini-vehicles that are smaller in size than standard cars and in most areas require no proof of parking on purchase. The law limits engine size to 660 cc for kei vehicles which means they cannot go much over 80km/ph (50 mph). However, built to the same standards of regular cars, they are more economic to drive, insurance and tax is cheaper, and their compact size makes them easy to park. They have long been popular in the country especially as the second family car, but Japan's depressed economy, the ever more stylish designs, a slight increase in size and improved safety features have finally moved mini-cars into the mainstream making them some of the best selling cars on the market. Buying a car used to be comparable to lifetime employment, one company for life. Car manufacturers produced cars that people could advance to as they reached the different stages of their life. As in other aspects of the new economy, this no longer holds true. The pre-bubble loyalties and alliances have all but disappeared as consumers seek what best serves their needs or what they can afford. For some this has meant forgoing ownership and using rental cars when necessary, for others mini-cars are the solution. Japanese car makers in the meantime are striving to stay one step ahead, focusing their energies on environmentally friendly vehicles. The hybrid car that can switch automatically between a petrol powered engine and an electric one has already hit the road and its low fuel emissions and unprecedented gas mileage are paving the way for cars of the future.

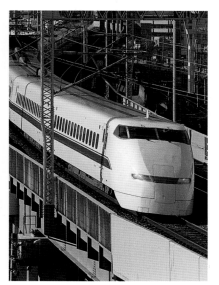

Despite the popularity of cars, bicycles remain a common means of getting around. As cars idle in traffic, cyclists weave their way through side streets. Salarymen suited up for work, before beginning their lengthy commute into town, may cycle to the local station then park in a huge lot solely for bikes. Mothers with children on their bikes shop for groceries, uniformed ladies sell miniature cartons of liquid yoghurt by bike and policemen patrol their local beat on two wheels. These bikes are not snazzy ten-speed racers or mountain bikes but bikes with at most three gears and a bell to facilitate manoeuvering through crowds.

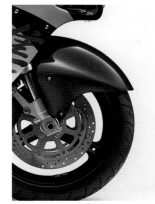

Given the density of Japan's urban areas, narrow roads and mountainous countryside, its mass transit systems are remarkable feats of efficiency and engineering that continue to be refined and improved.

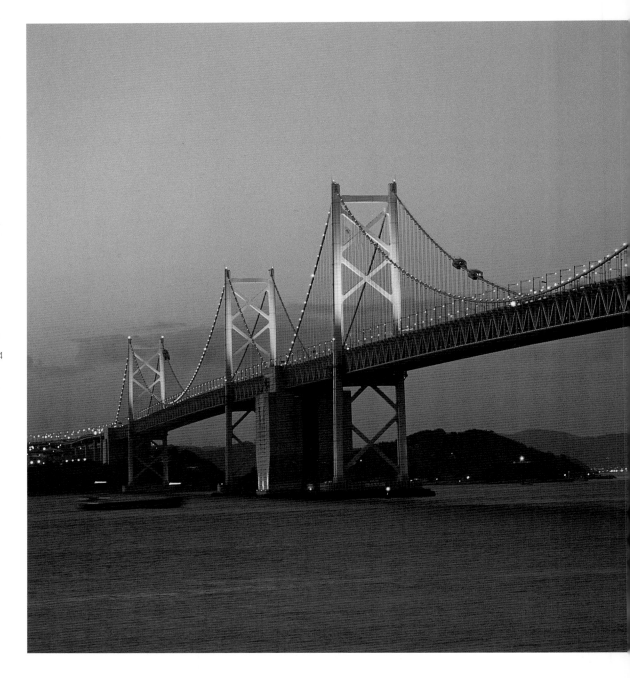

communication & packaging

advertising

homeware

products

124

transport

food & drink

interiors

architecture

fashion

communication & packaging

advertising

homeware

products

125

transport

food & drink

interiors

architecture

fashion

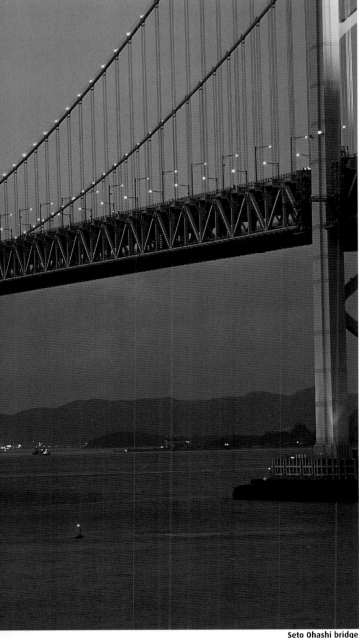

Seto Ohashi bridge

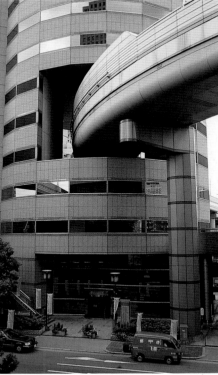

freeway exit ramp runs through office block

The Seto Ohashi bridge, which opened in 1988, is in fact comprised of six sections of bridge that span several small islands between the main island of Honshu and the island of Shikoku. Japan is prone to earthquakes and typhoons, therefore, the structure was built to withstand maximum wind resistance while the foundations of the bridge have been designed to accommodate the effects of seismic activity (an earthquake of up to magnitude 8.5). The double-decker construction of the bridge is the longest of its kind in the world with an upper level for cars and a lower level for rail tracks.

A lack of space and the huge expense of land has produced some innovative architecture and infrastructure in Japan. Homes are built to accommodate parking spaces that are carved out of the ground floor, roads are constructed above rivers and department stores have railway lines running through them. Suspended above the city, roads, railway lines and pedestrian bridges often overlap each other and as seen above a building has been specifically built to accommodate an elevated section of road.

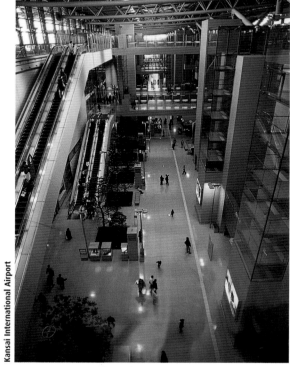

Kansai International Airport

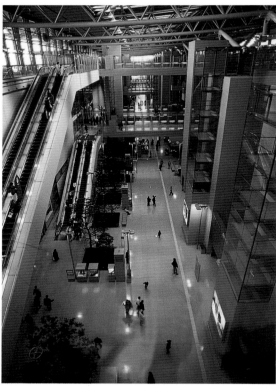

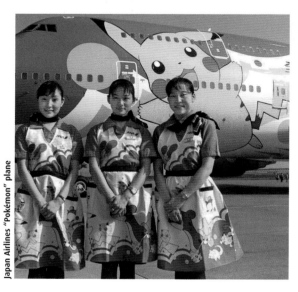

Japan Airlines "Pokémon" plane

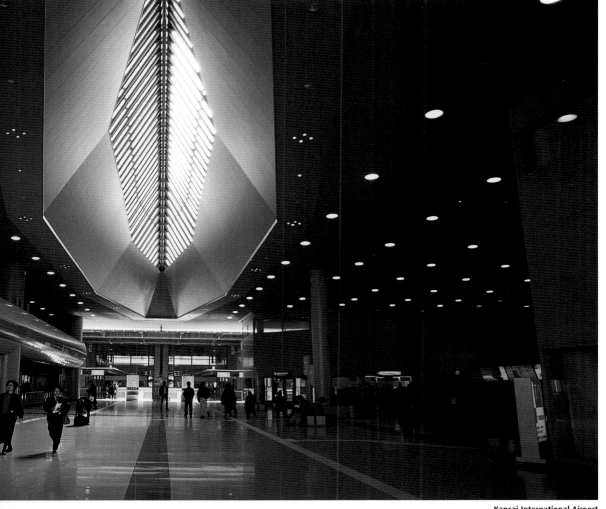

Kansai International Airport

communication & packaging

advertising

products

lifestyle

127

transport

food & drink

interiors

architecture

fashion

Up until the opening of Kansai International Airport in 1994, Narita Airport, located an hour's drive from Tokyo was the main artery for international air travel in Japan. Designed by the architect Renzo Piano, Kansai International Airport sits on an artificial island of reclaimed land in Osaka Bay and has proved to be a remarkable feat of civil engineering and design. The enormous glass and steel structure is built on piles driven through mud and into bedrock. Since settling is a major cause for concern on reclaimed land, the piles are continually monitored for excessive settling and where necessary recalibrated.

128

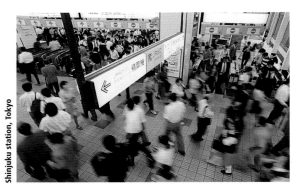

Shinjuku station, Tokyo

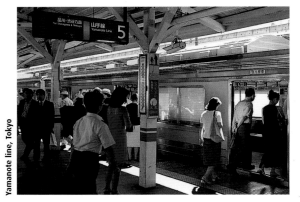

Yamanote line, Tokyo

With over two million passengers a day, Tokyo's Shinjuku station is the busiest in the world. Trains from the suburbs arrive packed with passengers who then thread through the station's corridors to connect with underground trains shuttling them in to downtown office districts. Japanese railway stations are unique in that many of them are lined with underground arcades and shopping malls often leading directly into a department store.

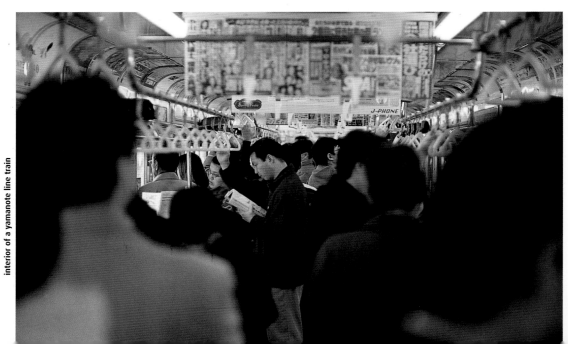

interior of a yamanote line train

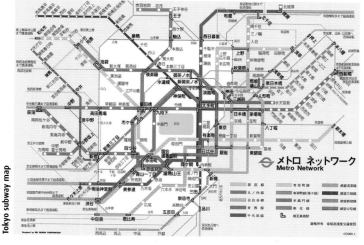

Tokyo subway map

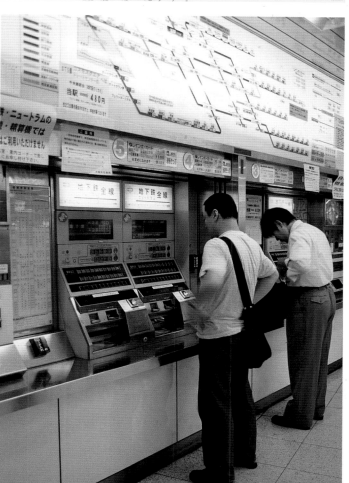

ticket vending machines

Walls of automated vending machines dispense tickets – complete with a computerized icon of a lady simultaneously bowing and saying thank you – and incomplete fares are also adjusted by machine at the end of a trip. Many trains now have computerized signs that announce the train's arrival at each station (both in Japanese and English) while some trains have miniature televisions built in to the walls of their carriage broadcasting the latest news.

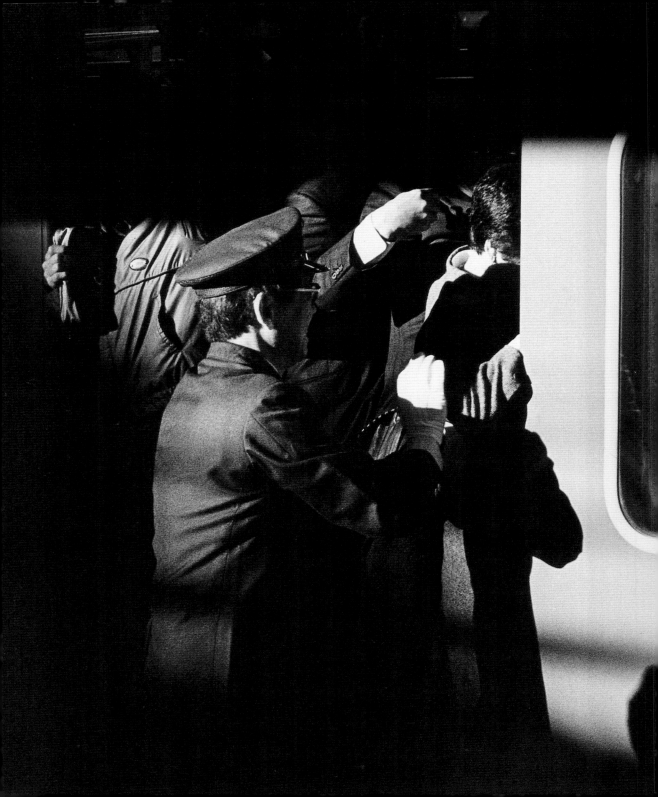

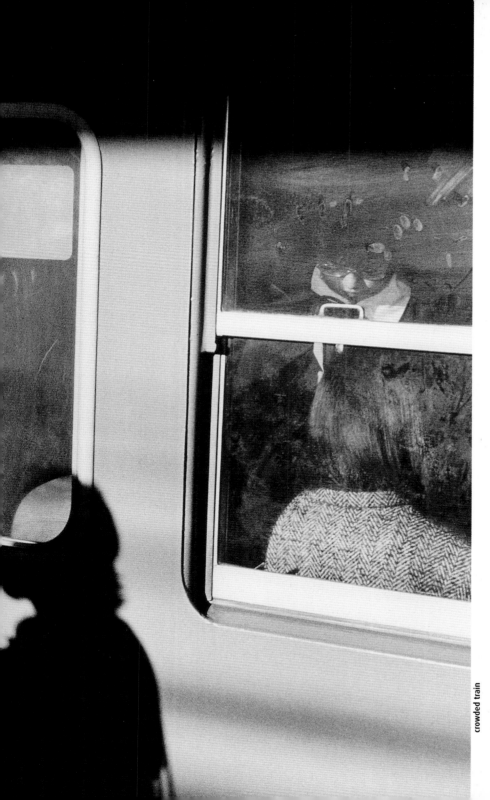

crowded train

At most busy train stations, it is customary for a uniformed employee to greet the train and to ensure that all passengers alight and board safely. Armed with a whistle, his job is facilitated by television monitors suspended from the ceiling showing different sections of the platform and occasionally a step is used to gain elevation to survey the crowds. Extra employees man the platform during rush hour to help squeeze passengers on board and ensure that no one gets stuck in the automatic closing doors.

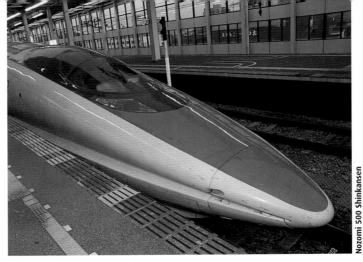

Nozomi 500 Shinkansen

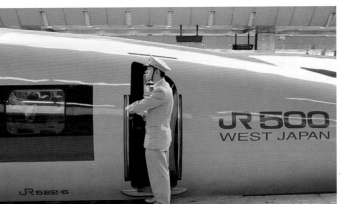

Shinkansen series 500

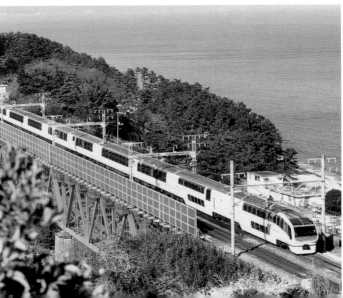

Superview Odoriko

Rail is generally the most efficient way to travel through much of Japan. High-speed *Shinkansen* services shuttle passengers in sleek trains the length of the country at speeds up to 300 km (185 miles) per hour. At the other end of the travel spectrum are special summer trains, furnished with tatami mats. On these, passengers sit cross-legged, eating and drinking and watching the world roll by at a more leisurely pace. The "Super View Odoriko", which runs along the coastline of the Izu peninsula, offers tiered seating at the front and back of its trains with seats designed facing outwards to the view.

The new designs of the Shinkansen trains with their long aerodynamic noses facilitate travel at high speeds which these days are maintained even while climbing steep gradients through Japan's mountainous regions. Future development for rail travel in Japan is focusing on linear rail technology with superconducting magnetically levitated trains. The Japanese and the Germans are currently in a race to perfect these innovations and be the first to launch this radically new means of travel.

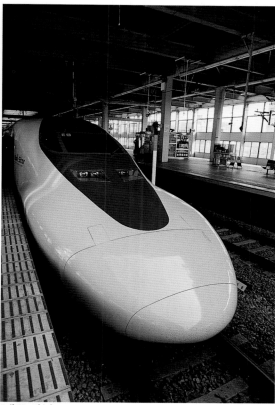

Rail Star Shinkansen

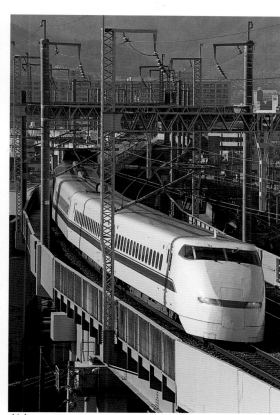

Shinkansen E2

communication & packaging

advertising

homeware

products

133

transport

food & drink

interiors

architecture

fashion

communication & packaging

advertising

homeware

products

134

transport

food & drink

interiors

architecture

fashion

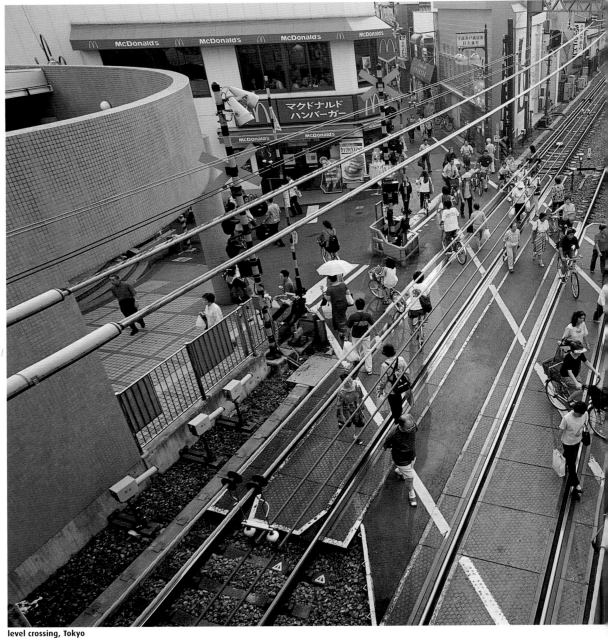

level crossing, Tokyo

communication & packaging

advertising

homeware

products

135

transport

food & drink

interiors

architecture

fashion

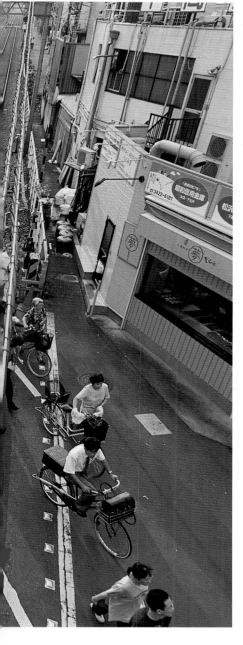

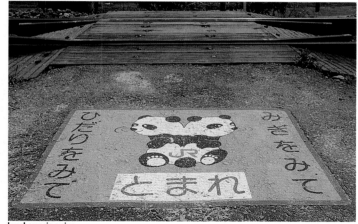

level crossing sign

Level crossings are an integral part of Japan's infrastructure. Although most of Tokyo's rail systems run quietly underground, the majority of commuter trains that leave the city run overground, their tracks winding their way between office blocks and businesses, crossing roads and working their way out to suburban neighbourhoods. This results in the curious scene of one of the world's busiest capitals being brought to a halt by the "ding ding ding" sound of a level crossing barrier going down, as the commuter trains barrel in and out of the city. The sign above appears on the road before the railway tracks, and cautions pedestrians to "stop, look left and look right" – the Japanese, like the British, drive on the left hand side of the road. Japan is full of visual guides to assist drivers and pedestrians alike. Mirrors on poles aid with blind corners, electronic boards on the toll-paying highways show which sections of the route are congested, while some traffic light signals now have a countdown sign to enable time-conscious pedestrians to see how much longer they will have to wait until the lights change – Japan is still a remarkably obedient country when it comes to traffic manners

communication & packaging

advertising

homeware

products

136

transport

food & drink

interiors

architecture

fashion

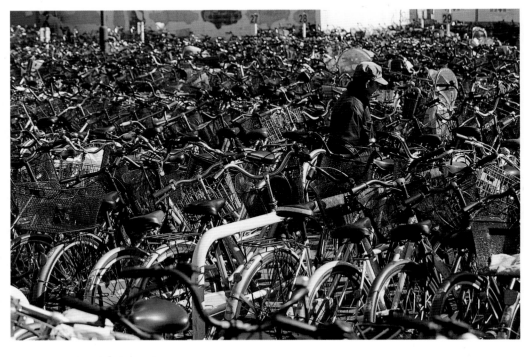

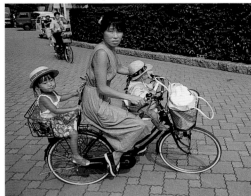

mother on bike with children

Unlike the lycra-clad cycle couriers on their multi-speed bicycles flying through Japan's downtown business districts, the average cyclist wears everyday clothes and rides a basic bike with three speeds at the most. A bell to alert pedestrians, plenty of baskets for a briefcase or shopping, and a couple of seats to carry the kids is the extent of the vehicle's accoutrements. Cycling is an incredibly practical means of transport, whether to get to the local station before a lengthy commute, or to carry out one's business, like the sight of an old man who carries around a block of ice on the back of his bicycle to deliver to clubs and bars for their patrons' evening drinks. At one time it was safe to leave one's bicycle unlocked, however, with an increase in crime, locks are now customary. One innovative accessory involves a remote sensor, which activates a red light on the bike enabling its location to be easily found – rather useful for the intoxicated salaryman – although most cyclists still seem to prefer the good old fashioned method of combing aisle-upon-aisle of identical looking bikes.

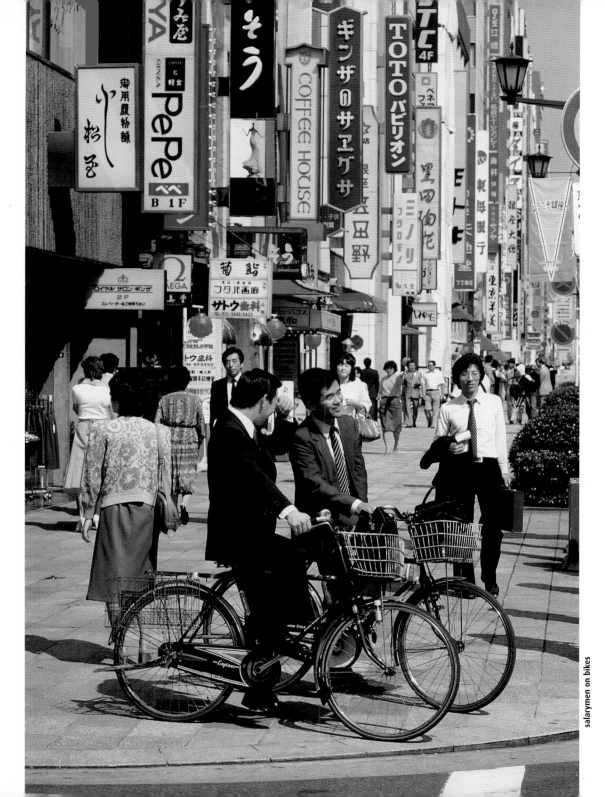

transport

communication & packaging

advertising

homeware

products

food & drink

interiors

architecture

fashion

salarymen on bikes

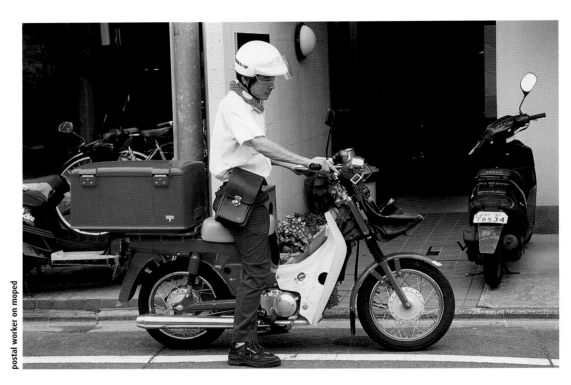

postal worker on moped

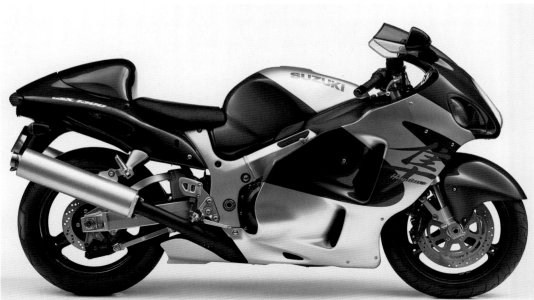

Suzuki Hayabusa motorbike

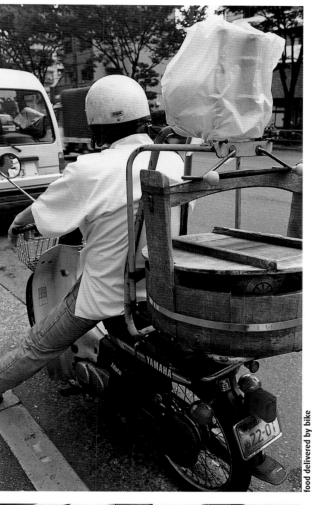

food delivered by bike

Japanese motorbike manufacturers such as Honda, Suzuki and Kawasaki have been instrumental in the development of the motorbike ever since the 1950s, introducing innovative technology that has revolutionized the industry. The Japanese pursuit of compact design combined with greater performance has featured heavily in the development of Suzuki's popular *Hayabusa* motorcycle shown opposite. Motorbikes are a popular mode of transportation for small businesses, in particular restaurants that offer home delivered food. One of Japan's ingenious inventions is the carrier attached to the back of the bike: loaded with springs and shock absorbers it allows trays of noodles in ceramic bowls to be delivered to a home without so much as a spill.

fast food delivery scooters

As a rule Japanese taxis are immaculately clean with their seats decked in white covers with lacy decorated head rests. Doors open and close automatically, which is extremely practical for a baggage-laden passenger. At one time taxi drivers were renowned for their smart uniforms, white gloves and caps but, just as the rest of the country seems to be adapting a more casual uniform, so many taxi drivers have quietly done away with their gloves and caps. Unlike Western addresses those in Japan usually have no road name and instead are assigned a series of numbers that correlate to specific areas. Since the number of the house is usually assigned in the order that it was built, finding an address is not a terribly logical exercise hence most Japanese resort to using landmarks as a means of directing a taxi driver to their destination.

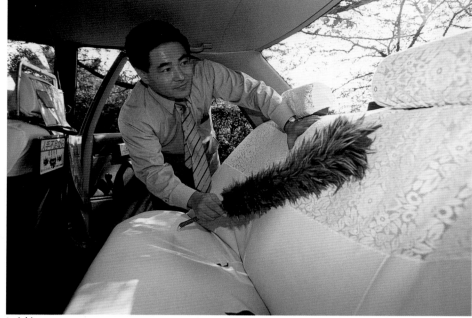

taxi driver

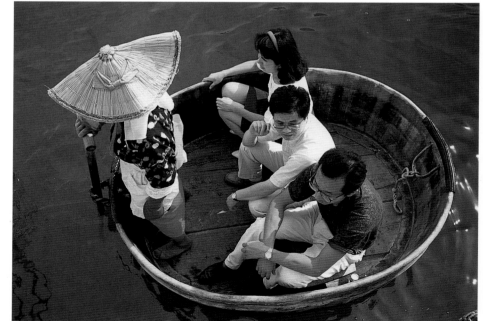

boating on Sado Island

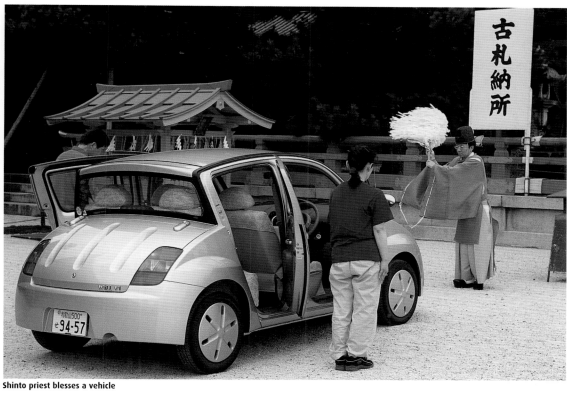

Shinto priest blesses a vehicle

communication & packaging

advertising

homeware

products

141

transport

food & drink

interiors

architecture

fashion

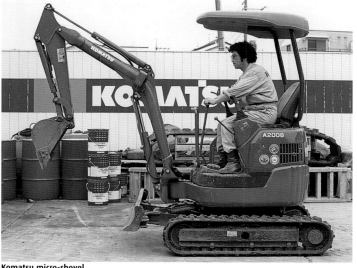

Komatsu micro-shovel

The Shinto blessing of a car is a common tradition for new owners to ensure safe driving and protection from traffic accidents. A cheaper alternative is to buy a colourful amulet from a shrine which is usually hung from the car mirror and ensures the same protection.

The design of the Komatsu digger is perfectly suited for Japan's narrow building plots and side streets where larger machinery may find it hard to manoeuvre. Attention to detail in Japan means it is possible to see workmen carefully placing pieces of carpet down on the road for the digger as it rolls by, in an effort to protect the street from unnecessary wear and tear.

communication & packaging

advertising

homeware

products

142

transport

food & drink

interiors

architecture

fashion

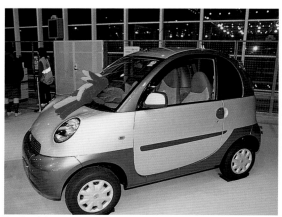

Toyota mini car

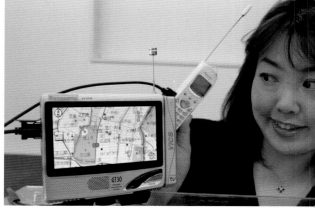

car navigation system

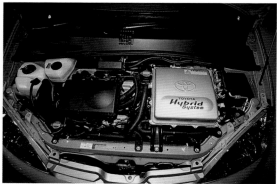

hybrid engine

While Japanese manufacturers have continually sought ways to make cars more compact, fuel efficient and eco-friendly, the latest development of the hybrid car is proving to be a major breakthrough. Unlike the electric car, which needs to be plugged in and charged, the hybrid car generates its own electricity through braking. Handling the same as a regular car, the hybrid car is powered by a combination of an electric motor and petrol engine, with a computer designating when the electric motor alone is sufficient and automatically switching between the two. These low emission hybrid vehicles, such as Toyota's *Prius* and Honda's *Insight* have already garnered numerous awards.

Many car makers offer navigation systems as additional options to their cars Functioning through a computer satellite these dashboard mounted navigators are able to offer directions and maps on a computerized screen. Internet access is also being added to these systems which will allow drivers instant access to information on restaurants, films and other events.

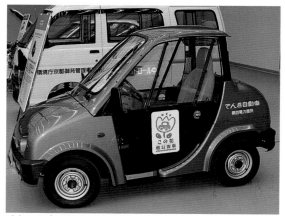

Mini-sway electric car

communication & packaging

advertising

products

behaviour

143

transport

food & drink

interiors

architecture

fashion

Just as the majority of Westerners would not think of putting mayonnaise on their pizza, they would be no doubt just as unlikely to purchase a car with the model name *Cedric*. Western names are often used for car models, however names that might appear unusual in the West are often totally appropriate in Japan. Manufacturers do change the names of their cars for the overseas market and have become more savvy to their international image, however as Daihatsu's name for its new mini van *Midget* illustrates, what would be a negative selling point in the West is often a plus in Japan.

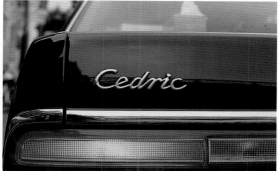

car names

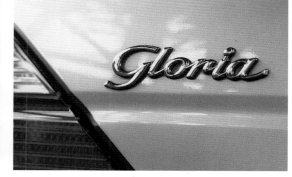

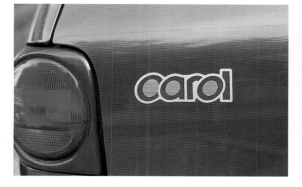

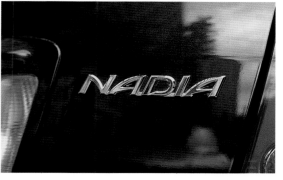

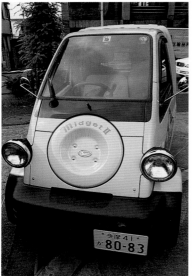

Midget II

Japanese cars are renowned for being reliable and economical to run as witnessed by the global popularity of Toyota's *Corolla* and the Honda *Civic* However, like many of Japan's mid-sized cars their design, for the most part, has been safe if not verging on boring and uninspired. Cars renowned for their classic design and style, such as Mercedes, BMW, Alfa Romeo and the new VW Beetle have all been top sellers among imported cars in Japan. In an effort to attract the discerning consumers in their late twenties and early thirties, Japanese manufactures have developed cars with more style and appeal such as Nissan's retro-looking *Figaro* and Toyota's *Will VI* car seen on page 141.

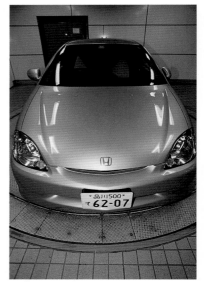

Honda

144

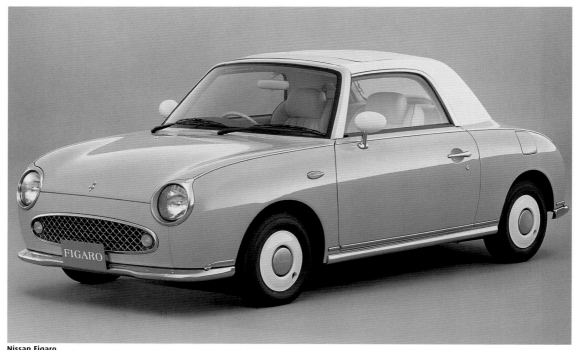

Nissan Figaro

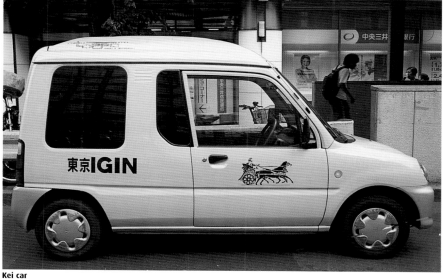

Kei car

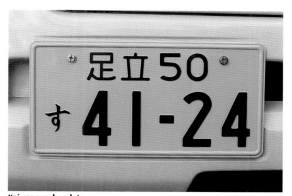

Kei car numberplate

Multiple car ownership is a trend that is increasing in Japan, with families opting for a standard sedan car for longer journeys and relying on a second mini car for short shopping trips. While standard white plates require proof of parking before purchase, the yellow *kei* plates do not. The compact size of these kei cars means they are easy to park and particularly suited to narrow roads, particularly in Japan's rural areas.

communication & packaging

advertising

homeware

products

145

transport

food & drink

interiors

architecture

fashion

communication & packaging
advertising
homeware
products
146
transport
food & drink
interiors
architecture
fashion

products

A wide array of electronic products such as flat screen televisions, digital cameras, PlayStations, DVDs, and ultra thin computers have come to symbolize Japan at the beginning of the twenty-first century, resulting in a country synonymous with innovative, high quality, cutting-edge design. Ironically, it was the aid of America in the depressed postwar years that kick-started Japan's manufacturing industry and subsequently contributed to its current position as the world's second largest economy.

In the late 1940s when the American occupying forces arrived in Japan, local manufacturers were called upon to cater to the Americans' lifestyle, epitomized by washing machines and refrigerators. As had been done almost a century before in the Meiji era, when the Japanese had feverishly set about emulating the West by building railways and steam engines, Japanese manufacturers again copied the design of these shiny new American products, perceived as symbols of ultimate sophistication in contrast to Japan's grim economy. These products were soon to be coveted by the Japanese housewife and in the 1950s, department stores began promoting a modern (i.e. Western) lifestyle that could be attained through the purchase of a television, refrigerator, and washing machine. Japan's long history of absorbing foreign influences, then refining and assimilating them in to their own culture saw the same principles applied in the manufacturing process. Bulky Western appliances and furniture were reduced in size and modified to fit the Japanese market. By the late 1950s, Sony had revolutionized this concept, reducing the television to a portable size and introducing a pocket-sized radio – both firsts of their kind.

These radical improvements in design and technology laid the foundations for the futuristic, innovative technology embodied by Japan's consumer electronics today. Though sparked by Western models, much of its design has roots in Japan's rich traditional arts and craft culture. The labour intensive, quality workmanship of the craftsman joins both functionality and beauty that originates in Japan's indigenous religion, Shintoism, the worship of spirits and gods found in the natural world. Reverent to nature, the craftsman seeks to reveal the true spirit of a material, whether it be wood, clay or metal, thereby enhancing its original beauty and dissolving any need to embellish. As these crafts today require time consuming domestic labour, they have now become items of luxury as opposed to the utilitarian role they once served.

At face value, modern industrial design can appear far removed from the traditional world but many of the functions revered in contemporary products, such as economy of

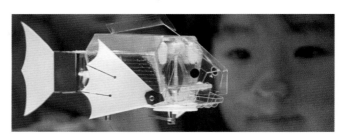

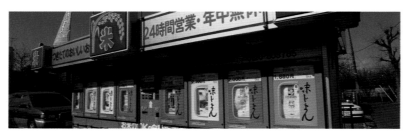

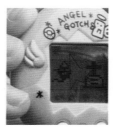

size, portability and multi-functionality are embedded in Japanese culture. For example the compact video camera with the viewfinder and screen that twists out while recording then folds seamlessly back into a compact unit, the camera with a sliding cover that once pulled back allows the lens to extend, or a miniature black manicure kit, concealed in a small flat case that slides open.

With limited space to house a desktop computer at home and expensive local phone calls, the internet did not take off in Japan as quickly as it did in the West. Instead the Japanese adopted cellular phones with miniature screens, now the most popular way to send and receive e-mail, yet another example of Japanese deftness to assimilate a foreign product and adapt it to their own needs. This strong cultural trait has sparked antagonistic views of Japan which has long been accused of appropriating ideas from overseas then refining them into superior products. Culturally, however, the traditional way of learning a craft has always been one of emulation: an apprentice observing a master, learning through osmosis as the student becomes familiar with the materials. Perfection for the craftsman was traditionally more about enhancing the natural beauty of a material rather than asserting the individual ego. Historically, craftsmen, each a specialist in their own field have worked together. For example, a lacquer bowl requires a woodworker to craft the bowl, then someone else to apply the lacquer. This ethos is seen in the world of industrial design where in-house design teams at large corporations such as Sony and Canon work closely with the technical side and the marketing division to produce innovative and style driven products representative of the company as a whole as opposed to any individual designer or developer.

Antithetical to the sleek and *oshibui* (astringent) is the love of kitsch best expressed by character goods and cartoon figures. While children carry Pokémon lunch boxes to school, teenage girls carry cellular phones around on a Hello Kitty band. Hello Kitty is so ubiquitous she appears on anything from slippers, chopsticks and sellotape dispensers to vacuum cleaners and even has her own car. Animal imagery is also rife in Japan, pandas, koalas and cats – the cuter the better – are recurring images often found on products, in particular telephone cards. Cuteness is not solely confined to female products, however, as men will quite happily tote pictures of Mickey Mouse on their ATM cards. In short, cuteness is a virtue in Japan and capitalized upon to promote a product whether it be a lunch box or a not so talented pop star.

The quality control that once was the pride of the nation has been questioned after a series of major corporate accidents and misrepresentations. Cost cutting and a work force that had ceased to value traditional work ethics were deemed the cause. It was once possible for a foreign student in Japan to furnish an apartment with electronic goods put out as waste. Today it is a lot harder to do so. People are more fiscally conservative and no longer are compelled to perpetually update goods.

Nevertheless there is a renewed appreciation by the young for the traditional world. The consumer boom of the 1980s was swiftly

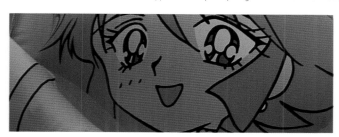

followed by a decade long recession. This has given the younger generation a new perspective on their own culture and a level of confidence that is enabling them to value and use the traditional arts and crafts as a basis for the creation of new design, once again producing something quintessentially Japanese.

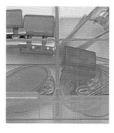
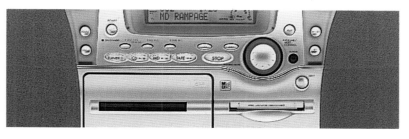

communication & packaging

advertising

homeware

products

147

transport

food & drink

interiors

architecture

fashion

communication & packaging

advertising

homeware

products

148

transport

food & drink

interiors

architecture

fashion

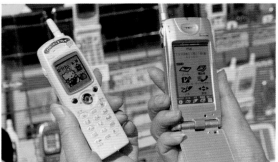

mobile phones

At one time public telephone calls were made with coins from cute pink, red and yellow telephone boxes that stood on shop counters. These were replaced by green push button phones that took telephone cards, although these are decreasing in number having been usurped by the cellular phone. Light and easy to use DoCoMo i-mode phones have proved to be particularly big sellers and internet access in Japan has soared through the use of mobile internet systems. Although internet usage on these phones is restricted to certain modified sites, mobile users can, for example, send and receive e-mail, trade stocks, book airline tickets or check film listings. Customized services such as the ability to download a graphic mascot, or a personal melody for incoming calls have proved extremely popular. Despite a tiny keyboard, users have become quite adept at thumbing through their messages and sending new ones, aided by pictographs such as happy faces, hearts, food or film projectors, and already the abbreviated language used in messages is beginning to make its way into everyday language. Worn on a rope around the neck or from a strap off the wrist, most cellular phones sport cute mascots not too dissimilar to the traditional religious lucky charms that many people carry in their purse or wallet.

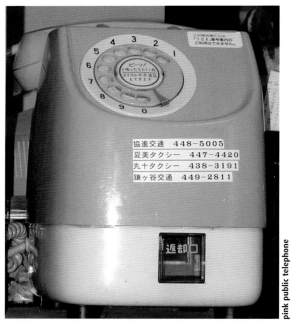

協進交通　448-5005
夏美タクシー　447-4420
丸十タクシー　438-3191
鎌ヶ谷交通　449-2811

pink public telephone

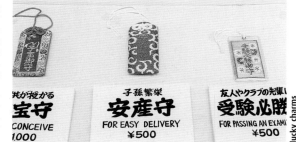

GOOD LUCK CHARMS

共が授かる
宝守
CONCEIVE
1000

子孫繁栄
安産守
FOR EASY DELIVERY
¥500

友人やクラブの先輩
受験必勝
FOR PASSING AN EXAM
¥500

lucky charms

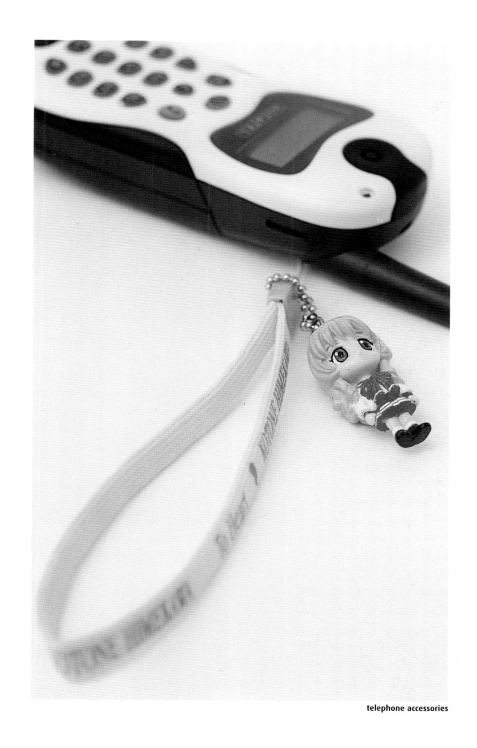

communication & packaging

advertising

homeware

products

149

transport

food & drink

interiors

architecture

fashion

telephone accessories

communication & packaging

advertising

homeware

products

150

transport

food & drink

interiors

architecture

fashion

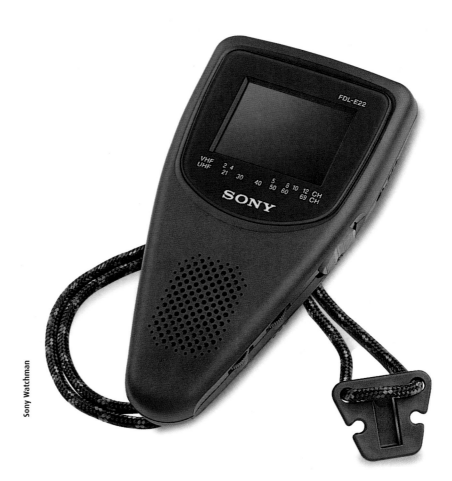

Sony Watchman

The concept of private space in Japan is very different from its perception in the West. In a nation where the group takes precedent over the individual, where employees work in open, cubicle-free offices and where parents may still share a bedroom with their children, privacy is something created mentally, rather than with actual physical space. As a result the Japanese have become adept at designing light compact products for the individual, that can be slipped into a pocket, hung off a wrist or around the neck – like Sony's television on a rope – and used wherever the user happens to be with little interruption to anyone else. This philosophy is what made the Walkman so successful and has fuelled the success of cellular phones and is what Sony is banking on in its launch of the Memory Stick Walkman, which can download and play audio files from the internet.

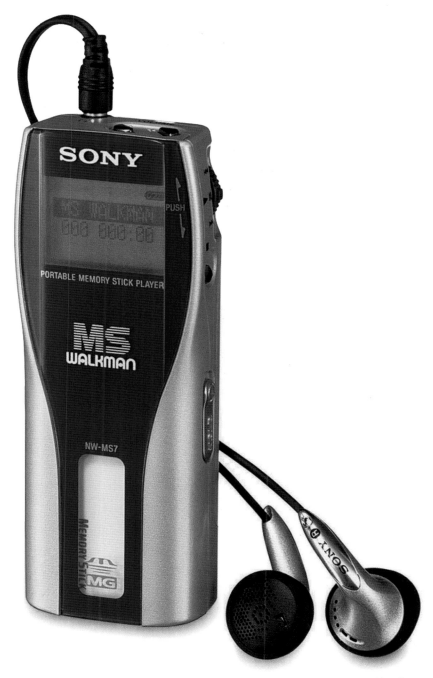

communication & packaging

advertising

homeware

products

151

transport

food & drink

interiors

architecture

fashion

Memory Stick Walkman

Puri Kura are miniature sticker photos taken at stand up photo booths that immediately became a huge hit with high school girls. Puri Kura – literally "print club" (*purinto kurabu*) – are one of Japan's many trends fuelled by high school girls. Ground zero is Tokyo's Shibuya district, home to arcades full of print club photo booths; trends here gradually make their way into the suburbs then across rest of the country. Each set of photos comes with a choice of different backgrounds and in a pack of sixteen, one to be stuck in a miniature Puri Kura album toted by every high school girl, the rest to be dispensed among friends.

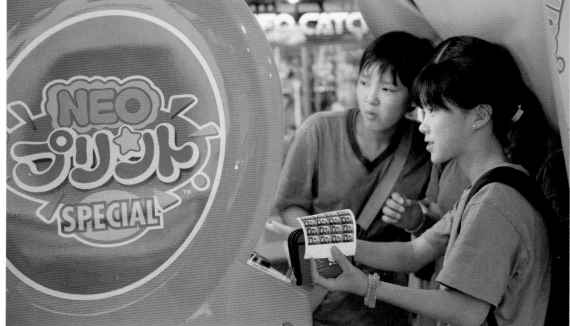

Neo-print photo booths

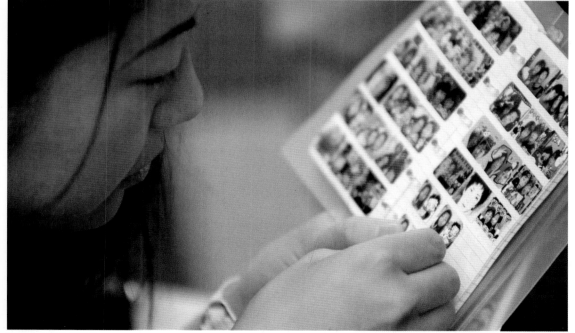

Neo-print photo stickers

communication & packaging

advertising

homeware

products

153

transport

food & drink

interiors

architecture

fashion

communication & packaging

advertising

homeware

products

154

transport

food & drink

interiors

architecture

fashion

The Japanese continually strive to make the smallest, most compact lightweight products such that the release of new products is ongoing. Occasionally certain classic designs come along, such as the Elf camera or the Canon Ixus (below), where the design can be little improved upon, only the technology updated. Even the old fashioned "boom box" has remained little changed and still sells well. Manufacturers will often offer a limited supply of a line in certain colours making the product somewhat exclusive but this policy also serves as a form of test marketing.

Casio has long been an innovator of fashionable watches, however, its popularity began to fade with the growth in the use of mobile phone usage. Watches were in danger of becoming redundant as mobile phones, often hanging from the wrist, became the easiest way to check the time. In an effort to combat this Casio developed new functions for their line of watches with a Wrist Audio Player that can play over 40 minutes of audio and can be heard with tiny plug-in earphones and a Wrist Camera that can store up to 100 images. The Instax Mini camera is unique in that it was designed expressly to appeal to high school girls. A sophisticated version of the Polaroid, only taking smaller sized photos, it became an instant hit.

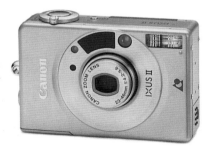

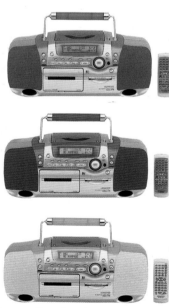

Rampage "boom boxes"

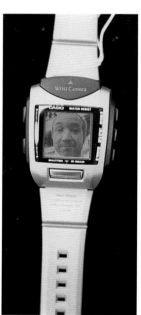

digital camera watch

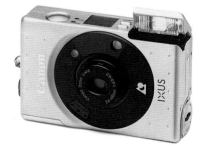

Canon Ixus camera

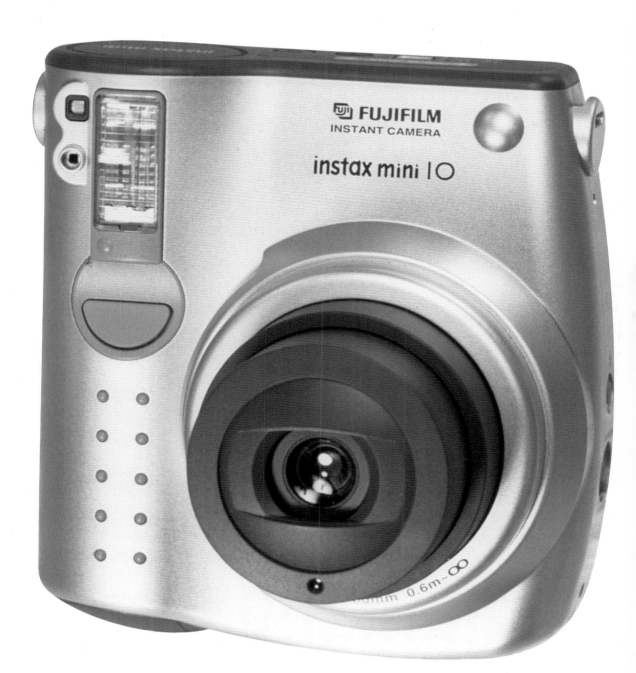

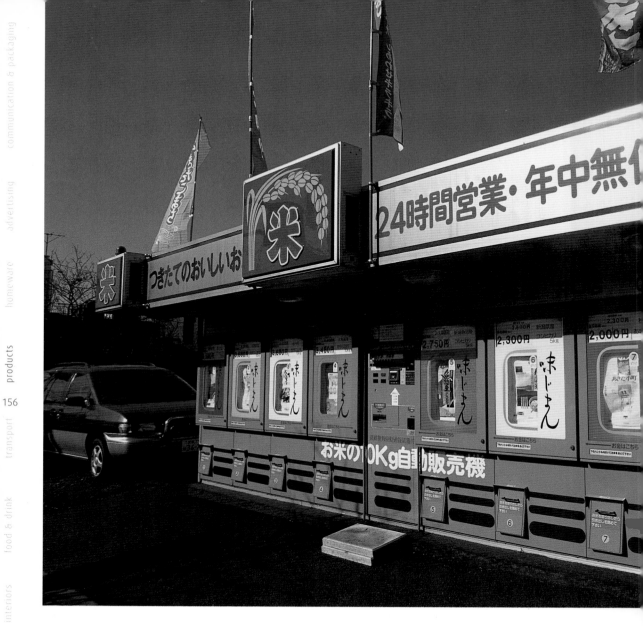

communication & packaging

advertising

homeware

products

156

transport

food & drink

interiors

architecture

fashion

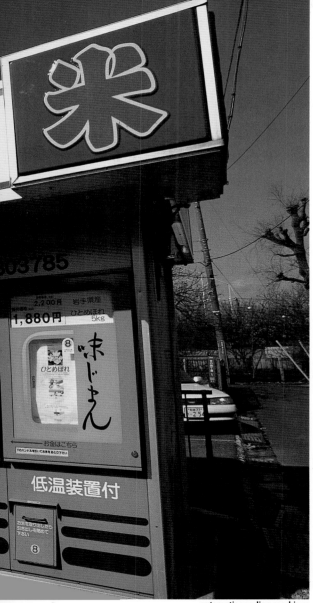

There are over five-and-half million vending machines in Japan selling everything from soft drinks to rice, as shown here. As the world leader in automated retailing, vending machines are ubiquitous throughout the country, lining city streets and appearing randomly on country roads: even Mount Fuji boasts a soft drink vending machine at its summit. Some machines are set up in rows like a miniature convenience store offering everyday staples like eggs and sushi. Consumer convenience is the main draw, hot tea and coffee in cans are sold in winter and cold drinks in summer. Instant noodles are dispensed from machines with hot water available at the push of a button, while other goods such as beer, whisky, underwear, socks, condoms, batteries, videos, pornographic magazines and cigarettes are also available. Some shrines even have vending machines to sell their *omikuji* (lucky fortunes). From a manufacturers' perspective, vending machines provide a great opportunity to advertise and test a product.

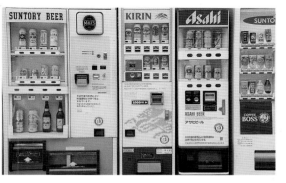

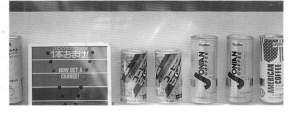

automatic vending machines

communication & packaging

advertising

homeware

products

157

transport

food & drink

interiors

architecture

fashion

Teen idol bands are big business in Japan and the ability to sing is less relevant than an ability to be groomed and packaged for the mass teen market. Shown here is one such band of girls that enjoys enormous popularity, Morning Musume. Since teen idol bands tend not to write their own songs, emphasis is on heavy styling and choreography, with cuteness the over-riding factor.

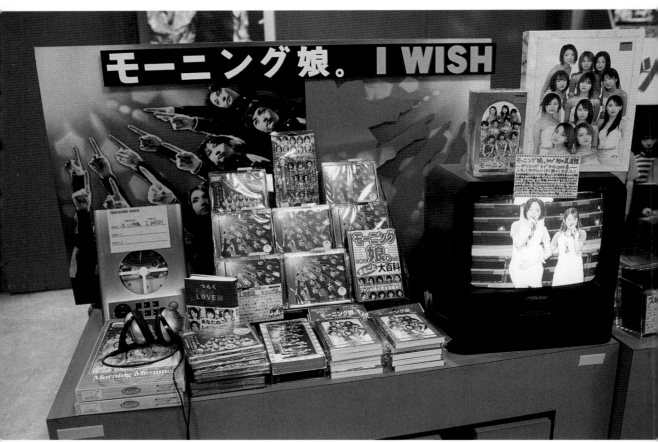

Morning Musume

For the past several years "100 yen" stores have been opening up in the heart of Japan's fashionable shopping districts. At one time the Japanese would have balked at being seen with shopping bags full of bargain goods but an ability to spend money carefully has become a virtue in post-bubble Japan. Filled to the rafters with a huge variety of goods, including an inordinate amount of plastic, these multi-level stores sell anything from kitchenware, stationery and make-up, each item for only 100 yen.

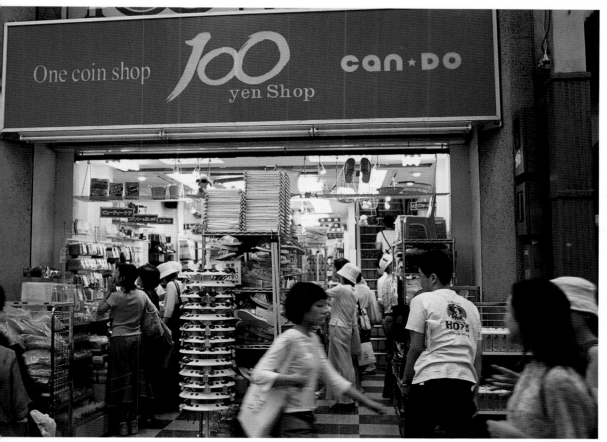

100 yen store

communication & packaging

advertising

homeware

products

160

transport

food & drink

interiors

architecture

fashion

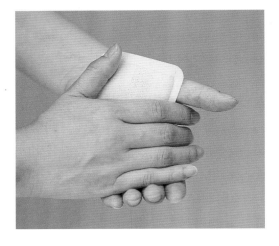

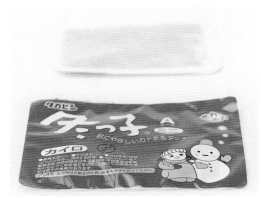

Hokairo handwarming packets

Although Western medicine is carried out by the majority of the Japan's doctors and hospitals, many people still have a healthy respect for Eastern medicine. The Japanese practice *shiatsu* massage, which focuses on the body's pressure points, as well as acupuncture. *Sentos*, Japanese public baths, usually offer vibrating massage chairs after a dip and there are a multiple of devices on the market for beating the back to relieve stress. One common approach is with magnets. Attached with sticking plaster, the magnets are placed on the body's pressure points to help align the flow of energy. Equally popular is the hot pack. Once removed from its wrapper it is rubbed together causing a chemical reaction that heats the contents. One side of the pack is self-adhesive allowing it to be stuck to the back and will remain warm for several hours rather like a hot water bottle. While the magnets tend to be used by the older generation, the young may often take hot packs when they go skiing and tuck them into their clothes.

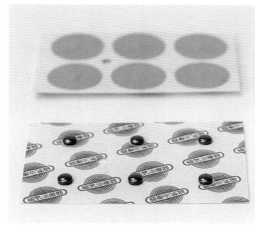

magnets

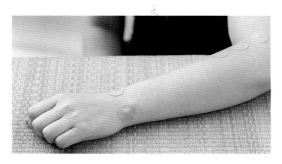

communication & packaging

advertising

homeware

products

161

transport

food & drink

interiors

architecture

fashion

Bunbougu is the Japanese word for stationery and is another area where Japanese design, with its attention to detail and love of the miniature, excels. Miniature paper clips, pins, rings and bindings are produced in a variety of colours with miniature stacking cases in which to store them and cute pencil cases bearing character goods, filled with sparkling pastel coloured pens are part of every school bag. Plus Corporation designed the Team Demi portable desk set shown on this page in 1984, and it rapidly became a bestseller. There have since been copies of the original design, but none that have surpassed this classic.

Team Demi desk set

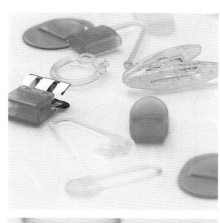

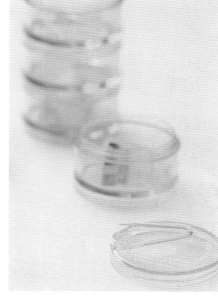

stationery kit

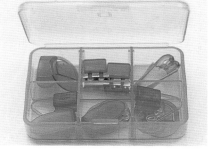

communication & packaging

advertising

homeware

products

163

transport

food & drink

interiors

architecture

fashion

communication & packaging

advertising

homeware

products

164

transport

food & drink

interiors

architecture

fashion

With the launch of its PlayStation Sony took what was essentially a toy and launched it into the world of multimedia entertainment. It proved an instant hit and its successor PlayStation (PS2) has since flown off the shelves scooped up by eager teens ready to try out new game titles on the sleek black box. Like most Sony products it is multi-functional, incorporating both a CD and a DVD player and internet access is imminent. Sony has also developed a portable version of the PS2, PSone that is a third of its size and can access the internet via cellular phone.

A huge trend was fuelled by high school girls with Bandai's virtual pet, Tamagotchi. A colourful hand-held case housed a virtual animal that required constant care and attention from virtual feeding to cleaning, to enable it to grow and be happy. Other virtual pets such as Angel Gotch have failed to replace the original popularity of Tamagotchi although the Lovegety enjoyed moderate success with its key ring, that once programmed to seek a karaoke partner or love interest, beeps when someone of the opposite sex bearing the same interest comes within a ten metre range.

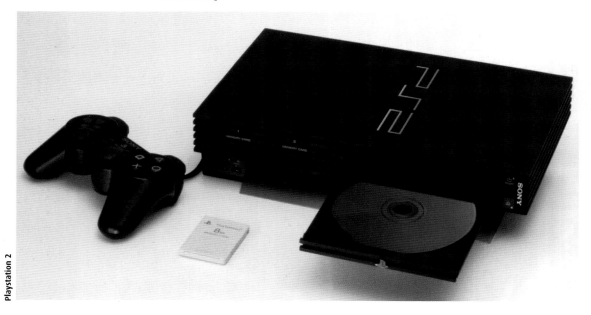

Playstation 2

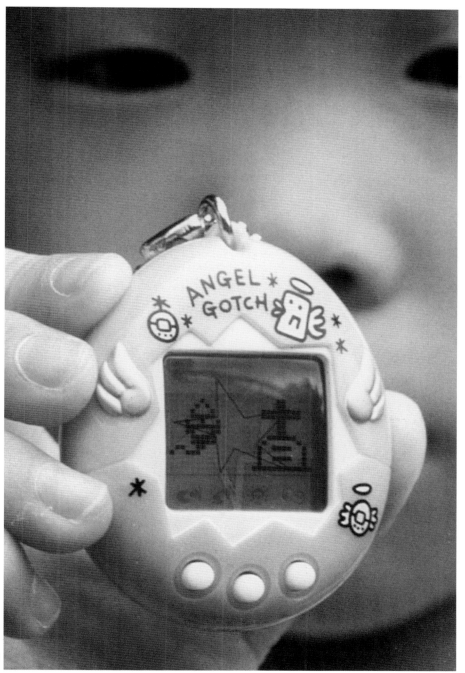

Angel Gotch

communication & packaging

advertising

homeware

products

165

transport

food & drink

interiors

architecture

fashion

communication & packaging

advertising

homeware

products

166

transport

food & drink

interiors

architecture

fashion

Japan has had a long running interest in robots. Efficiently incorporated into car and other production lines for some time, robots are currently under development for such diverse consumer uses as aids for the aged. Robot updates continually announce the development of new talents such as the ability to dance, speak, and even serve wine. At one time confined to industrial use, robots are now enjoying huge popularity in the consumer electronics market as robotic pets. In a country where cuteness is a valued asset and animation and *manga* (comic books) are an integral part of popular culture, robots are not only made to look human or pet like, but their inventors have bestowed these machines with human qualities. In the wake of the success of virtual pets, robotic pets are only a natural extension. Sony's Aibo – a play on the Japanese word for partner which also stands for Artificial Intelligence Robot – responds to treatment by its owner through a sensor. Like a real dog it can wag its tail, lie down and roll on command as well as respond to other orders. Following the popularity of Aibo, other pets are being marketed including Cookie, a hamster robot, Sega's Poo-Chi robotic dog and Takara's fish robots.

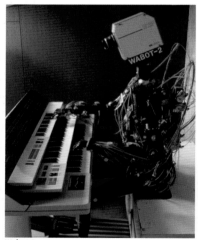

Wabot 2

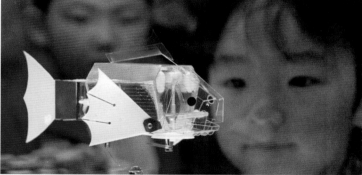

fish robot

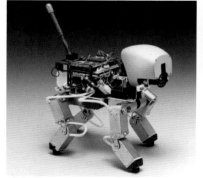

robot cat

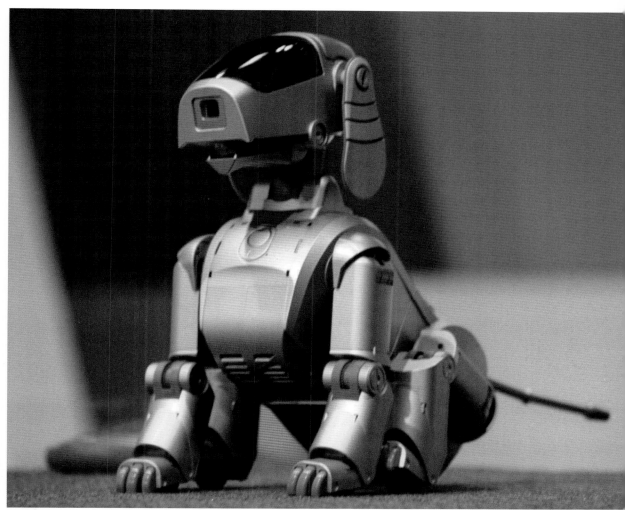

Sony Aibo

communication & packaging

advertising

homeware

products

168

transport

food & drink

interiors

architecture

fashion

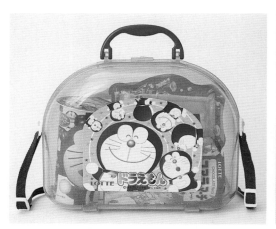

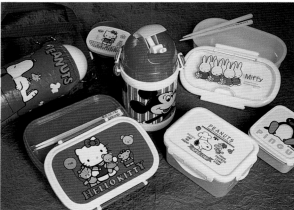

Japan is a nation saturated in images and the pictorial nature of *kanji* only adds to the Japanese appreciation of the visual. Manga, animations and character goods are prolific throughout the country. Although highly popular with children and teens, manga are also read by adults, just as many of the popular character goods have a cross-generational appeal. Many of Japan's early animation and manga figures are still popular today and include "Atom Boy", "Doraemon" and "Sailor Moon", although newcomers such as "Pokémon" and the more recent "Digimon" have firmly established their place on the animation scene. Character goods are a huge business in Japan and the rest of Asia where they have a large following. Sanrio, the character goods company that puts cute images on lunch boxes, notebooks and stickers, earns almost half of its revenue from "Hello Kitty" alone. Each of its characters (with names like "Spottie Dottie", "Tuxedo Sam" and "Picke Bicke") comes complete with a biography: for example, many fans may be unaware that Kitty, celebrated her twenty-fifth birthday in 2000, and lives in London with her twin sister Mimmy.

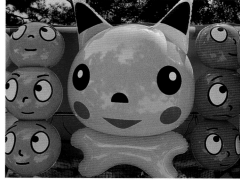

cartoon-inspired character goods

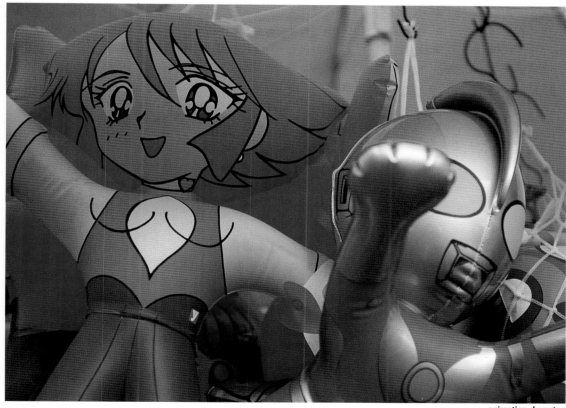

communication & packaging

advertising

homeware

products

169

transport

food & drink

interiors

architecture

fashion

animation characters

communication & packaging

advertising

homeware

products

170

transport

food & drink

interiors

architecture

fashion

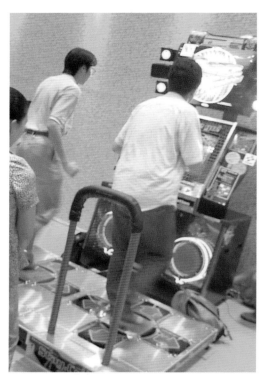

Dance Dance Revolution

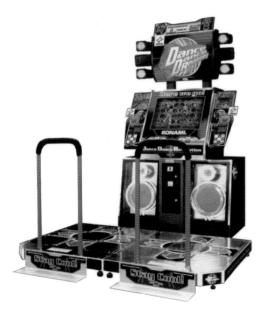

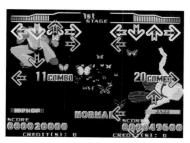

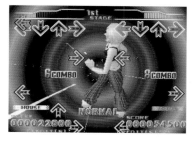

Dance Dance Revolution

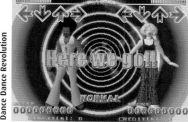

communication & packaging

advertising

homeware

products

171

transport

food & drink

int cars

architecture

fashion

The general perception is that the Japanese are by nature a rather shy, reticent nation. The commercial success of karaoke and the latest popular amusement "Dance Dance Revolution" (DDR) seem to indicate otherwise and the latter takes the level of exhibitionism seen in karaoke to new levels. The dancer selects a tune then instructions appear on the screen in the form of arrows. These correlate to four large arrow panels on the floor of the machine which the dancer is meant to follow. The steps becoming increasingly complicated the more proficient the dancer becomes. Konami, the makers of DDR discovered that young people found the dance game to be a great way to socialize and subsequently gave the machine two dance floors so players can dance alongside each other to the same tune.

communication & packaging

advertising

homeware

products

172

transport

food & drink

interiors

architecture

fashion

homeware

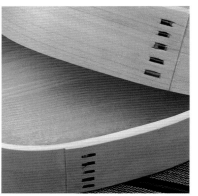

Before the advent of the Second World War, the majority of Japanese households relied on traditional handmade products and utensils, many of which had been passed down through generations. In the postwar years, as Japan embraced the West, these items were slowly replaced with mass produced plastic goods. In a contemporary home, although bamboo sieves and tea strainers, baskets for serving tempura and wooden saucers are just as likely to coexist with plastic rice paddles and chopsticks, and soup bowls coated to resemble lacquer ones, this shift towards mass production has had the effect of turning the handcrafted item, once a utilitarian tool, into more of a luxury item.

As a small country with a dearth of natural resources, Japan offers a surprisingly wide variety of handcrafted goods. Isolated from the outside world for long periods, the Japanese became deft at designing products with limited materials, coming up with ingenious applications in the process and they are renowned in particular for their pottery, lacquerware, metalwork and textiles. Many of these products are still made by hand today using age-old techniques. Lacquerware is one of the country's oldest crafts, lacquer being an extremely practical way of treating wood. It is derived from the sap of the *urushi* (lacquer) tree, which grows in Japan, although most raw lacquer today is imported from China. Like all traditional handmade products, lacquerware is an immensely time consuming and laborious process which requires the preparation and drying of wood followed by numerous coatings of lacquer. Once applied the lacquer strengthens the wood and protects it from rot and corrosion and also serves as an insulator for heat. Lacquer is used for many products such as trays, soup bowls, plates, chopsticks, water carriers and pouring bowls, all of which are still produced today, although in far smaller quantities than in the past.

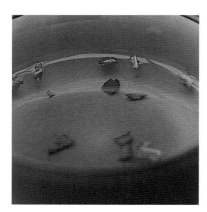

Another dominant craft is metalwork, evidence of which can be seen in the huge array of Japanese tools: kitchen knives, fish knives, vegetable knives, eel knives, cleavers, chisels, saws, planes, flower clippers, pruning scissors and so on. Originally metal was used for early farming tools, pots and swords. As craft tools developed they had to be small and easily portable since there were many itinerant workers. Today Japanese chefs still depend heavily upon a wide variety of traditional knives and kitchen tools.

Japan's ceramic tradition is one of the oldest in the world and pottery is still very much in use in the average home. Japanese cuisine relies upon the use of a variety of dishes and bowls which has kept this craft alive. A rich volcanic landscape offers a huge diversity of clays that are used to produce three main styles of ceramics: glazed stoneware, unglazed stoneware and porcelain. The latter is a more refined style often delicately painted while stoneware is rougher and thicker in stark contrast to the uniform image of Western china and its matching patterns. The Japanese craftsman has always worked close to nature embodying both a spiritual and organic element into a work. Asymmetrical pottery pieces are admired for their natural beauty and accidents in firing and imperfections are left as part of the design. As previously shown, the Japanese reverence for purity, simplicity and functionality is what is sought in the creation of pottery and this is seen not only in the texture of materials but also in the design. A pouring bowl with a slight indentation in the side for the thumb allows for an easier grip while another on the rim serves as a subtle spout.

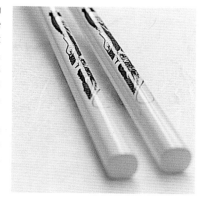

All of these crafts were standard homeware at one time and life in today's modern home is not too dissimilar to the old way of life in the country. The clay floored kitchen, at the same level as the outdoors was invariably a small area for the washing and preparation of food with a *kamado*, a wood fired clay stove for cooking. Clay pots sat on top for boiling, steaming and simmering food. The adjoining room was usually a raised wooden floor with an *irori* at its centre. The irori, a sunken clay pit filled with ash and a charcoal fire, was the centre of the household where the family would gather seated on the floor, both to eat meals and keep warm. Suspended from a beam above the fire was a wooden pole with an iron hook and a metal kettle attached. The kettle would be kept filled ensuring a constant supply of hot water while the steam would serve as a humidifier in the dry winter climate. Above the fire, also suspended, was a wooden platform used to smoke and dry foods.

The current "LDK" (Living, Dining, Kitchen) layout of a contemporary home follows this traditional style, with preparation of food done in a kitchen that seems rather cramped by Western standards, then served in an adjacent dining room. The kamado has been replaced by a stove that usually has only two gas rings and a grill which may appear primitive to the Westerner accustomed to an in built range and oven, however, baking is not typically part of Japanese cuisine so there is no tradition of an oven. If the need for baking arises such dishes (usually Western) are either cooked in a microwave, some of which can switch to an oven function, or in an oven toaster, where the settings are read not according to temperature but rather by food type: toast, pizza, gratin, sponge cake and cookie.

Although gas stoves and electrical gadgets crowd most contemporary kitchens, there has been a quiet revival of the kamado. Throughout its history, Japan, has managed to hold on to its own culture just at the point when it was in danger of disappearing. In the postwar years when the country embarked upon mass modernization, the Government concerned for the future of traditional crafts, endorsed a programme recognizing traditional crafts and artisans, bestowing the title of "Living National Treasure" upon them, a tradition that exists today. The continuation of traditional arts such as ikebana, the tea ceremony, noh and even geisha have also helped to keep these traditions alive.

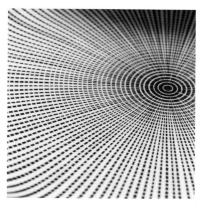

The current dilemma is whether the perpetuation of these crafts will continue. An average apprenticeship lasts for ten years and is time consuming, repetitive and laborious, little suited to the majority of young people, many of whom prefer to have part-time jobs rather than full-time employment. A lengthy economic recession in an economy that no longer guarantees lifetime employment has caused a small few, who at one time would have shunned taking over the family business, to reconsider as certain crafts and industries are on the verge of extinction. How these young differ from their predecessors lies in the fact that they not only wish to continue a craft that has enjoyed centuries of tradition, they are also beginning to seek ways to incorporate time honoured skills into a modern aesthetic, making them more relevant to contemporary living.

communication & packaging

advertising

homeware

products

173

transport

food & drink

interiors

architecture

fashion

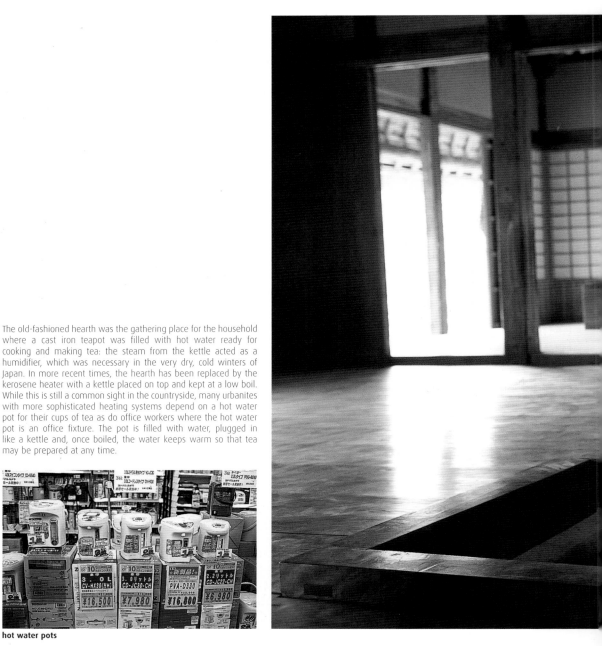

communication & packaging

advertising

homeware

products

174

transport

food & drink

interiors

architecture

fashion

The old-fashioned hearth was the gathering place for the household where a cast iron teapot was filled with hot water ready for cooking and making tea: the steam from the kettle acted as a humidifier, which was necessary in the very dry, cold winters of Japan. In more recent times, the hearth has been replaced by the kerosene heater with a kettle placed on top and kept at a low boil. While this is still a common sight in the countryside, many urbanites with more sophisticated heating systems depend on a hot water pot for their cups of tea as do office workers where the hot water pot is an office fixture. The pot is filled with water, plugged in like a kettle and, once boiled, the water keeps warm so that tea may be prepared at any time.

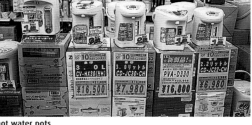

hot water pots

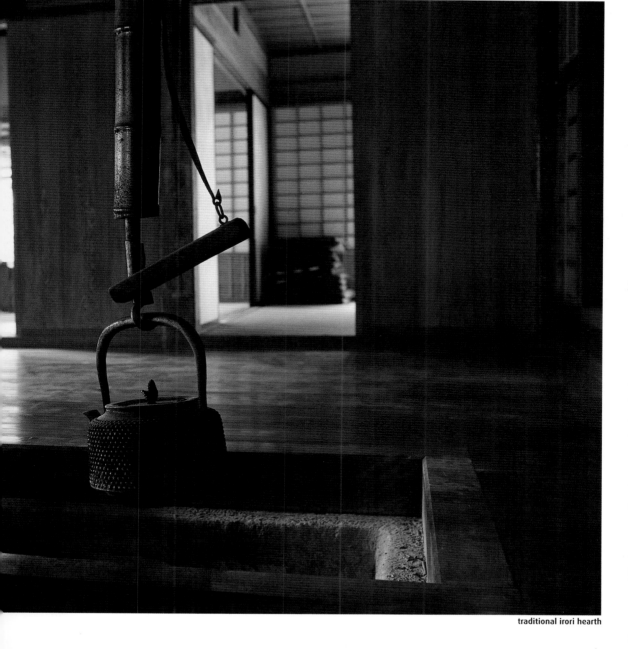

traditional irori hearth

communication & packaging

advertising

homeware

products

175

transport

food & drink

interiors

architecture

fashion

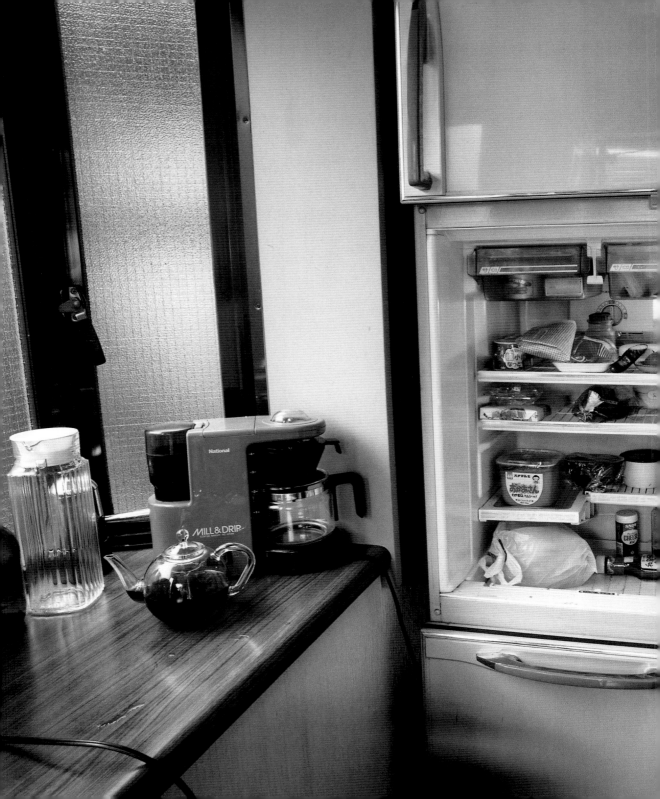

This Japanese fridge houses the staples of a modern Japanese diet: a tub of miso, pickles, *natto* (fermented soya beans), milk, eggs and other popular items such as Kewpie mayonnaise and Bulldog sauce – the latter used for *tonkatsu* (deep-fried pork).

The oven toaster is the Japanese equivalent of an oven and is standard fare in most kitchens, cooking anything from a slice of toast to a small gratin dish or mini pizza.

Invented in the 1950s by Toshiba, the design of the rice cooker has changed little since. Its functions have however, become increasingly sophisticated aided by "fuzzy logic", enabling rice of different types and amounts to be cooked at the right level.

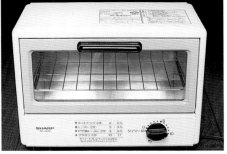

oven toaster

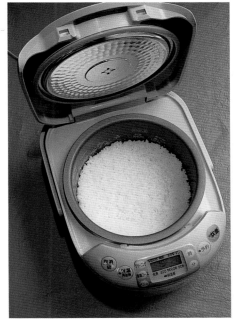

electric rice cooker

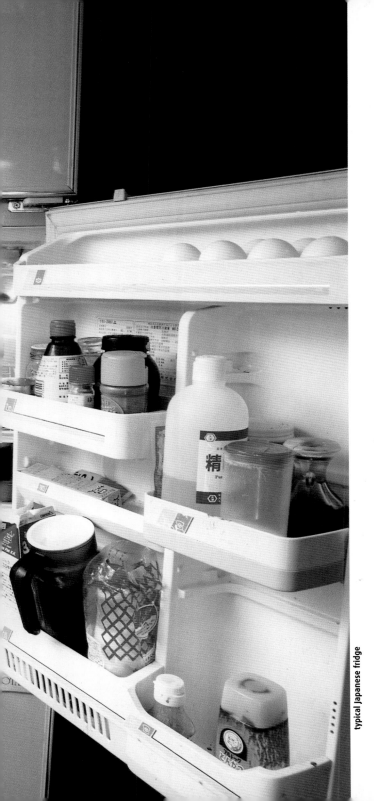

typical Japanese fridge

communication & packaging

advertising

homeware

products

177

transport

food & drink

interiors

architecture

fashion

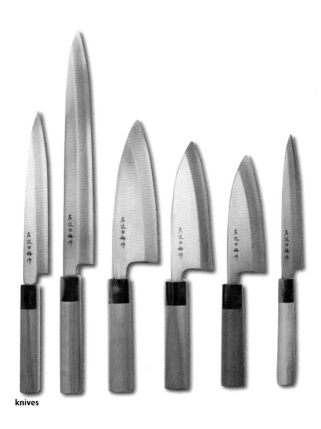

knives

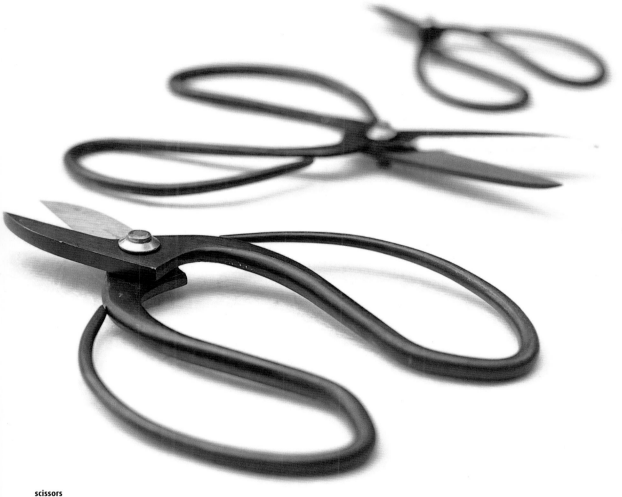

communication & packaging

advertising

homeware

179

products

transport

food & drink

interiors

architecture

fashion

scissors

Japanese carpenters have a sacred reverence for their tools and the same can be said of Japanese cooks. Knives come in a variety of sizes and are divided according to what is to be cut – typically vegetables, meat and fish. Japanese knives have a cutting edge on one side of the blade only, making them far more efficient than their Western counterparts. The scissors above are only one of several types used for flower arranging, although different schools tend to have particular allegiances. Other tools used in flower arrangement and bonsai include a variety of shears, snippers, sickles and scythes.

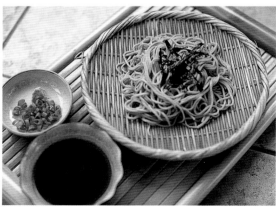

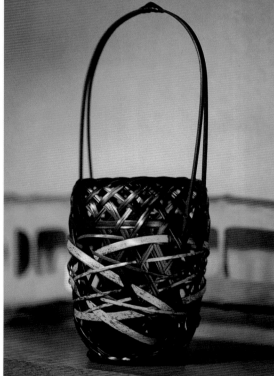

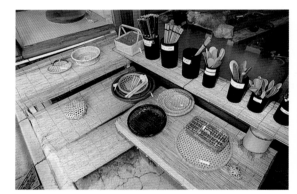

communication & packaging

advertising

homeware

products

180

transport

food & drink

interiors

architecture

fashion

Bamboo is an extremely versatile wood – flexible, light and durable, there are over six hundred different varieties in Japan alone. Its uses range from the highly utilitarian to intricate works of art and it is seen in architecture, in the building of fences and as window blinds. Used in the making of paper lanterns, fans and traditional umbrellas, bamboo is also woven into fish baskets, winnowing trays and large baskets that are strapped to the back and used for carrying goods. Most homes, no matter how modern, own some form of bamboo ware, whether it be delicate forks used to eat Japanese sweets, a basket for serving tempura or small everyday saucers and mats. The tea ceremony has enjoyed a long tradition of using finely handcrafted bamboo goods, ranging from the whisk used for the preparation of tea to the simple beauty of finely handwoven bamboo vases.

bamboo goods

communication & packaging

advertising

homeware

products

181

transport

food & drink

interiors

architecture

fashion

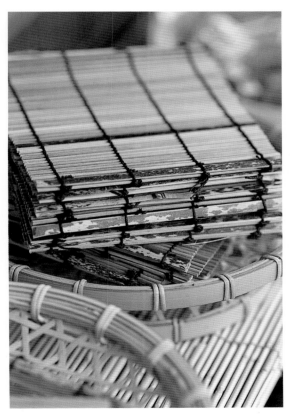

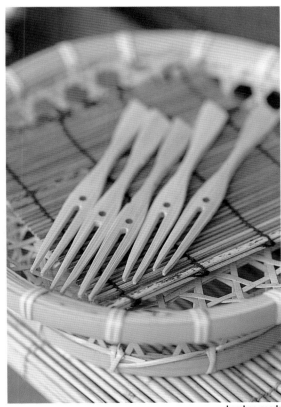

bamboo goods

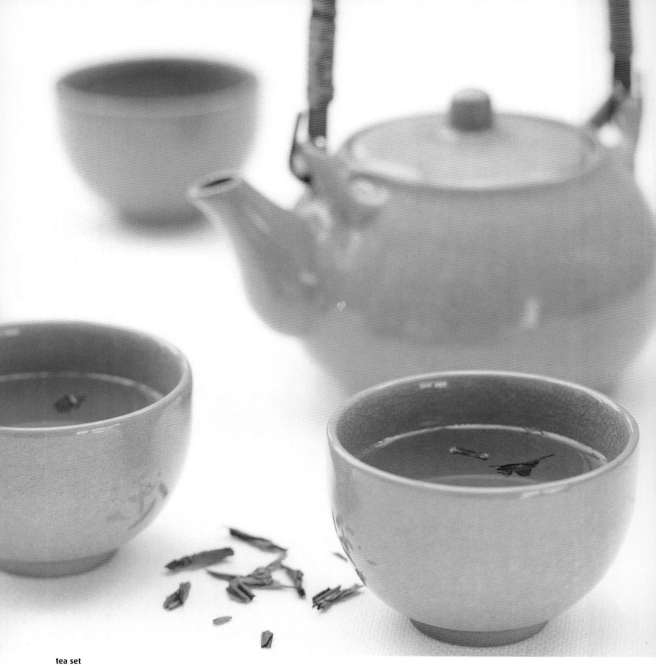

tea set

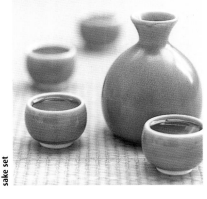

sake set

The glazed ceramic teacups shown opposite are typical in that they have no handle and are intended to be cupped in one hand, the other serving as a flat base like an improvized saucer. Cups and bowls tend to be sold in sets of five as four is believed to be an inauspicious number. The handle on a Japanese teapot is noticeable for the fact that it can be replaced, although more lavish teapots have carefully twisted wooden twine handles that are works of art in themselves. Just as a traditional home is noted for its tactile nature, Japanese cups and bowls are designed to be held and experienced and not just visually appealing. Sake cups and bottles come in a variety of shapes and sizes. Coloured glass cups may be used for chilled sake in summer, while thick, earthenware cups pair well with a hot sake in winter.

communication & packaging

advertising

homeware

products

184

transport

food & drink

interiors

architecture

fashion

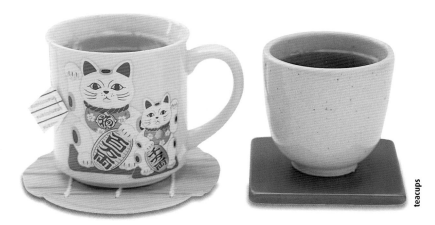

teacups

The *maneki neko* (lucky cat) with the raised paw is part of Japanese folklore. Frequently seen in shop windows or at the entrance of a house, a raised left paw is believed to encourage business while a raised right paw symbolizes prosperity. Shinto, Japan's indigenous religion, coexists naturally with Buddhism and most families combine aspects of both in their lives so that many homes have a Buddhist altar as well as talismen from a Shinto shrine. Often placed beside these objects will be a vermilion red papier mâché doll known as a *daruma* (opposite). With a weighted base that always rights itself, daruma come with no eyes. The purchaser makes a wish to the gods while painting in one eye, usually at the beginning of the year and, should the wish come true, the second eye is painted in. daruma vary in size but tend to get bigger as one ages.

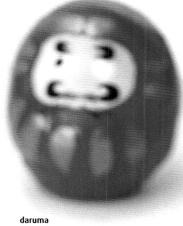

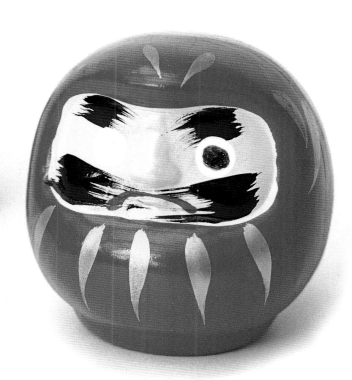

daruma

communication & packaging

advertising

homeware

products

185

transport

food & drink

interiors

architecture

fashion

communication & packaging

advertising

homeware

products

186

transport

food & drink

interiors

architecture

fashion

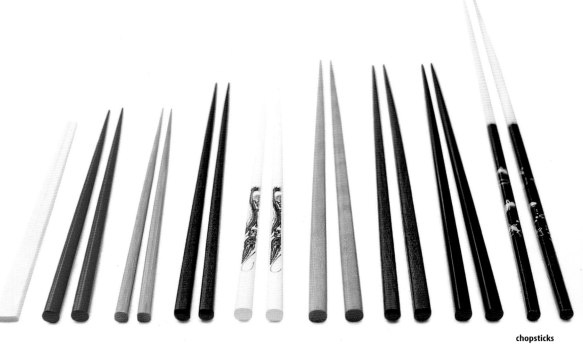

chopsticks

communication & packaging

advertising

homeware

products

187

transport

food & drink

interiors

architecture

fashion

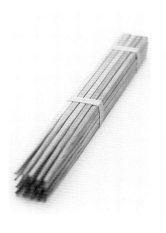

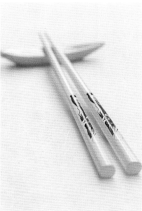

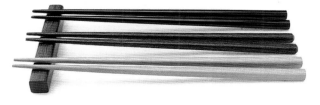

Japanese food is typically served in small-sized morsels with meat or chicken chopped into small cubes or sliced, almost sashimi-like to enable the use of chopsticks. Originating from China, Japanese chopsticks have pointed ends that taper: they are commonly made from wood and range from expensive lacquer-coated ones to plastic ones that slide into the lid of a bento box. Most Japanese cook with extra-long chopsticks, usually conveniently tied together at the end by a piece of string to prevent them coming apart. *Hashi-oki* are chopstick rests that range from the simple wooden blocks to more elaborate porcelain shapes depicting fish, flowers, cranes and fans.

188

While Western tableware emphasizes uniform patterns. Japanese dishes are selected according to how the food will best be presented. While many dishes are served in individual portions, large plates are used for ingredients such as sashimi, which is often arranged like delicate flower petals and a group of people will each take turns to help themselves. On formal occasions, when taking from a communal dish, it is polite to use the other ends of the chopsticks for picking up food, reversing them to eat.

plates

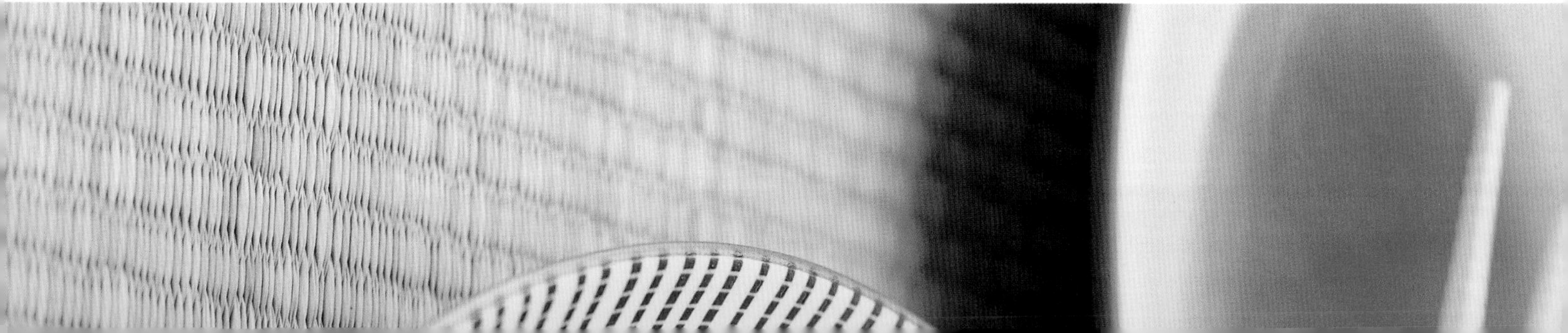

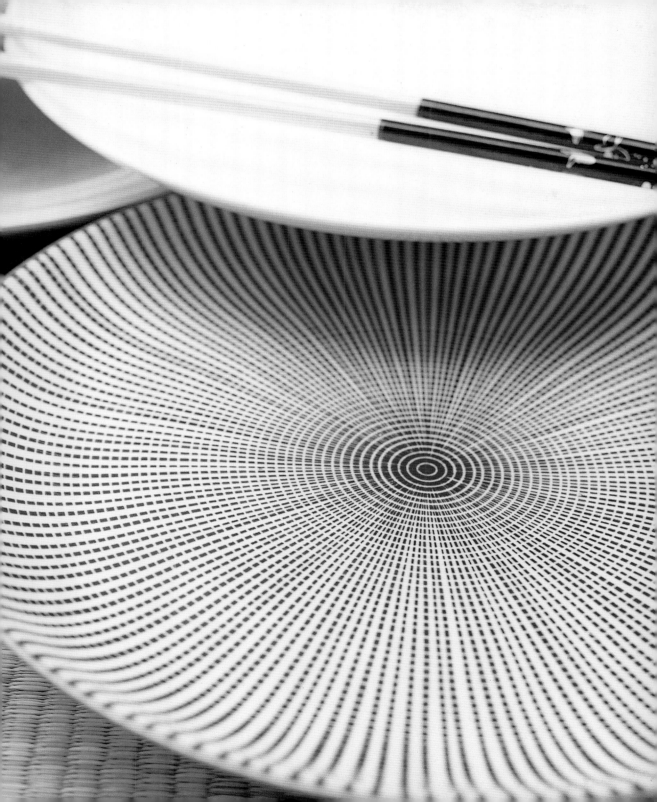

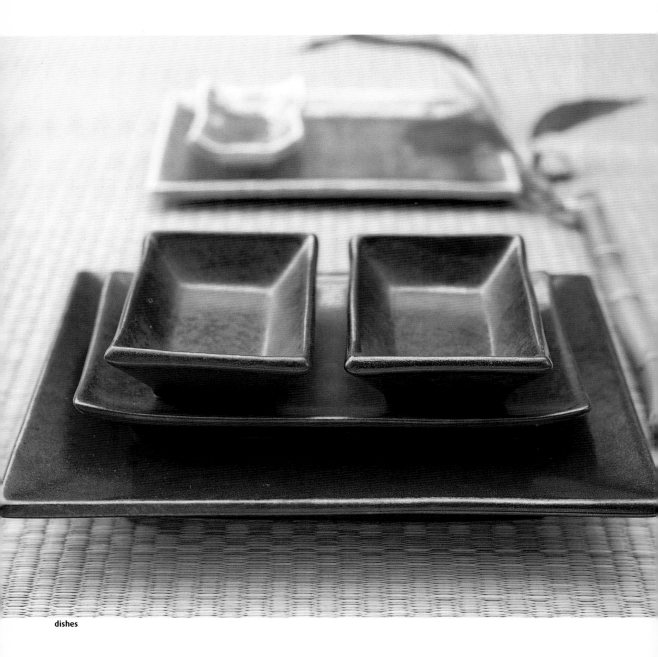

dishes

communication & packaging

advertising

homeware

products

transport

food & drink

interiors

architecture

fashion

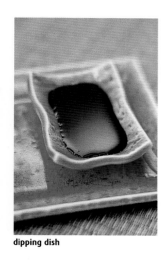

dipping dish

Sauces are an integral part of Japanese cuisine and small dipping plates are a common accompaniment. Like every other receptacle on the table, these are chosen to form part of a greater aesthetic experience. Just as the seasons are reflected in the food, so the tableware is selected accordingly. While foods are carefully selected to provide a balance of taste and texture, the appropriate vessels are required to provide a visual composition of the meal. The asymmetry reflected in Japan's arts and crafts as well as in the world of Buddhism is very much evident at the table. Different textures are mixed with various shapes, each contributing to the overall impression. Although the average meal at home does not usually include such an elaborate display of dishes, many more tend to be used than in a Western home.

communication & packaging

advertising

homeware

products

192

transport

food & drink

interiors

architecture

fashion

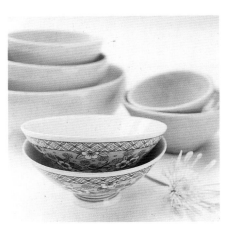

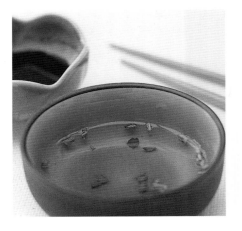

communication & packaging

advertising

homeware

products

193

transport

food & drink

interiors

architecture

fashion

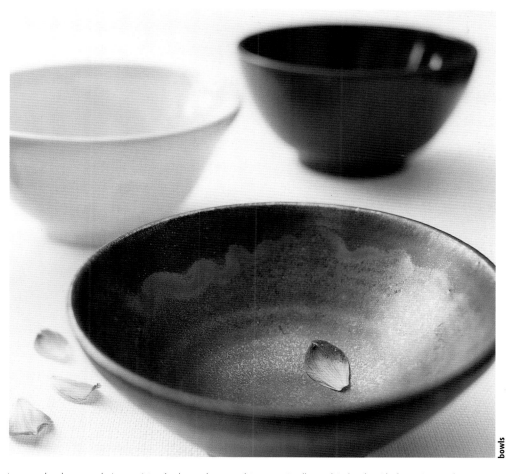

bowls

Japanese bowls are made in a variety of colours, shapes and textures. Small porcelain bowls with decoration on the exterior are used for rice, their size allows them to be held up to the mouth easily in one hand while the other feeds with chopsticks. The unglazed bowls, rough to the touch on the exterior, have painted glazed interiors perfect for displaying food. This aesthetic is typical of a restrained Japanese sensibility where less is more. Like a sombre coloured kimono with a brilliant coloured interior, Japanese bowls or pots often appear subdued on the exterior but may display ornately painted interiors revealed only once a lid has been removed. Each of the large bowls show variations in colouring; to the Western eye this would appear as an imperfection whereas in Japan this is seen as part of the natural process of creation.

communication & packaging

advertising

homeware

products

transport

food & drink

interiors

architecture

fashion

194

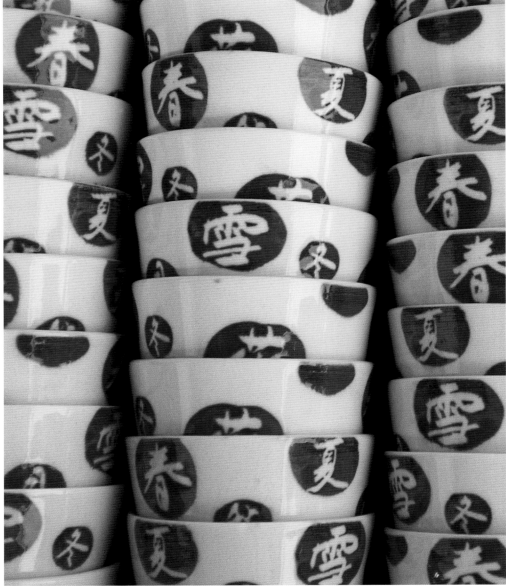

bowls

195

Cramped living quarters have produced a nation where a premium is placed on compactness as is seen in traditional tableware. Small trays used for dining fold and stack neatly upon each other, while bowls are often designed to fit seamlessly inside each other. While the West sometimes puts its china on display, the Japanese keep out what is necessary for everyday use, storing the rest. These more expensive items are often kept in nondescript wooden boxes, the only hint of what lies within, given away by the brightly coloured ribbon that keeps the lid in place.

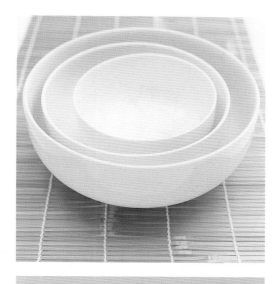

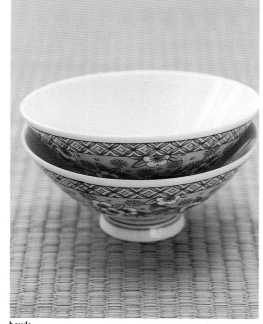

bowls

communication & packaging

advertising

homeware

products

196

transport

food & drink

interiors

architecture

fashion

Lacquerware is one of Japan's oldest craft traditions and is a labour-intensive process, beginning with the making of a wooden core, which is created by a specialist. This is then handed over to a craftsman for several layers of lacquer coating. The number of layers differs according to region, as do the different styles of decoration, which may range from gold leaf, mother-of-pearl inlay to a coloured lacquer painting design. Most homes own some form of lacquerware and if not used on a daily basis it is brought out for special occasions such as New Year. Miso soup is typically served in lacquer bowls, however these days, only the more exclusive restaurants use real lacquer while the rest depend on imitation lacquer bowls as shown opposite.

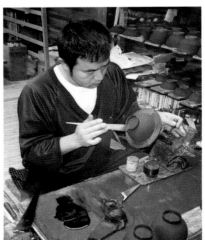

lacquerware

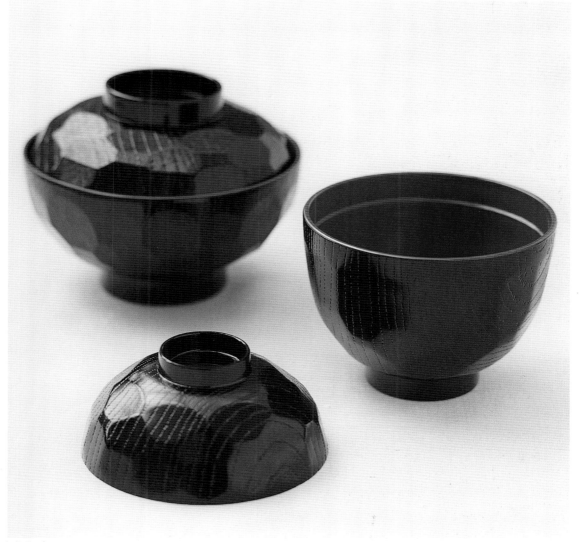

imitation lacquerware

communication & packaging

advertising

homeware

products

197

transport

food & drink

interiors

architecture

fashion

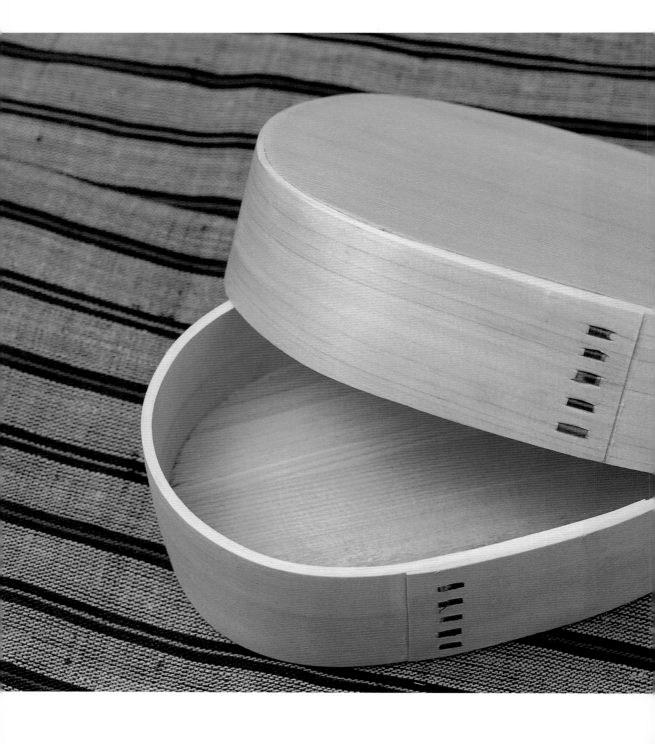

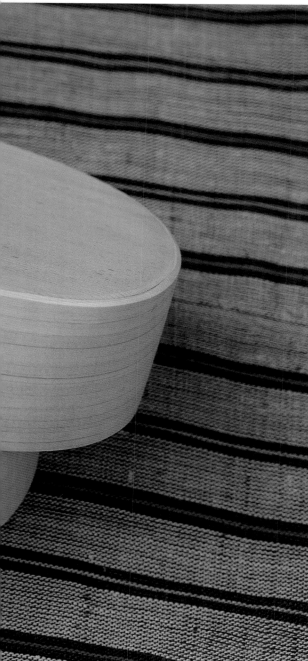

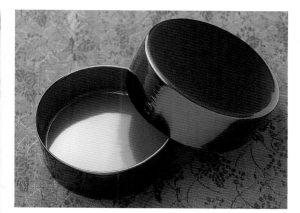

Both of these lunchboxes are made using a technique called *mage-mono*, a process that bends the wood. Typical woods used are cypress and cedar, as they are renowned for their distinctive grains. The wood is split into thin sheets, exposing the straight grain, then is immersed in boiling water before it is bent into shape. This process is repeated numerous times until the wood is suitably fashioned. When it is dry, the joints are pinned together with a strip of cherry bark. A lacquer finish will often allow the grain of the wood to be revealed and while it maintains the simple beauty of its form, it loses the scent and flavour of the wood, which is one of the charms of the plain wooden lunchbox on the left.

bento boxes

communication & packaging

advertising

homeware

products

transport

food & drink

interiors

architecture

fashion

199

communication & packaging

advertising

homeware

products

200

transport

food & drink

interiors

architecture

fashion

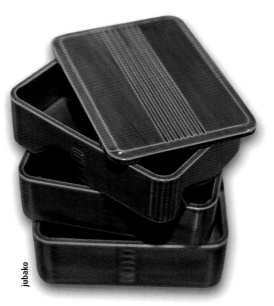

jubako

Jubako are tiered boxes that are used for formal meals, particularly New Year's celebrations. On this occasion, special dishes are prepared ahead of time with each food endowed with symbolic meaning – such as wealth and long life – and served in jubako. Traditionally, this was meant to allow a three-day break from cooking. Today many people find the preparation of food itself to be overwhelming and turn to department stores for their *osechi ryori* (New Year food), the price and contents of which determine whether or not the jubako is lacquered or a contemporary equivalent.

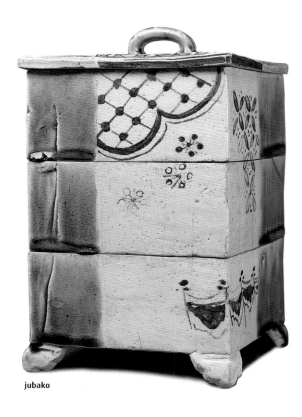

jubako

communication & packaging

advertising

homeware

products

transport

201

food & drink

interiors

architecture

fashion

communication & packaging

advertising

homeware

products

transport

food & drink

interiors

architecture

fashion

advertising

The world of Japanese advertising reflects a cutting-edge, technology driven nation with a constant flow of images and information around the clock. Early forms of advertising first appeared in the Edo Period (1603–1868) and are attributed to the theatrical world of *kabuki*. Its immense popularity turned the actors into arbiters of style during this period with many trends in kimono dress originating from kabuki. Popular actors were featured in colourful *ukiyo-e* woodblock prints along with the name of a product. They also appeared in fliers, a means of advertising in Japan that is still popular.

During this same period *furoshiki*, pieces of cloth used to wrap goods, began to bear store logos and acted as a form of advertising as merchants transported goods between cities. Edo shopkeepers also used logos to advertise their stores which they placed on *noren* – the cloth curtains hung on a pole over the shop entrance: this form of advertising is still prevalent today, mostly in restaurants. In Kyoto where there has been some attempt to minimize the use of neon, noren have been adopted not just by traditional eating establishments but by a wider range of shops, including contemporary stores.

The Japanese are an aesthetic nation and their reliance on visual cues and symbols parallels their keen attention to the seasons. The fabric and design of a kimono changes, regardless of the weather, to symbolize the arrival of a new season in spirit if not in fact. Such seasonal images are also a recurring theme in advertising. For several years a major railway company ran a successful campaign showing exquisite traditional images of Kyoto and other destinations in each season. With the simple English copy "Discover Japan" each image conveyed a strong sense of longing for traditional Japan. These visual cues rely on a common understanding and shared experience but to an outsider may appear elusive.

Advertising in Japan today is ubiquitous, ranging from the esoteric to the purely kitsch. The aforementioned reverence for the seasons is counterbalanced with an equal reverence for the artifice: flashing neon lights, monumental television screens adorning the fronts of buildings, subway cars lined with posters, illuminated shop signs and twenty-four-hour vending machines; the latter causing

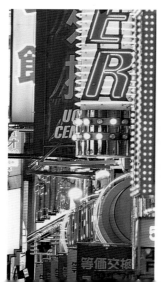

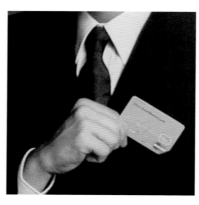

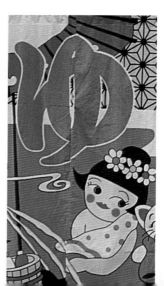

recent national concern due to the amount of electricity consumed by the millions of vending machines that line the nations' highways and byways. The urban dweller is not only mired in visual chaos but endures a barrage of noise. Automated rail ticket machines play a recorded "thank you" and simultaneously show a lady bowing. The *yakiimo* vendor sells hot sweet potatoes from his truck, accompanied by an automated cry. Traditional street vendors, once commonplace, are slowly disappearing, however, their shouts and hawking of goods have moved to urban retail centres. Cries of *irrashaimase* (welcome) greet shoppers, and are most vociferous in the basements of department stores where food stall clerks vie for customers.

For many years television commercials have featured Westerners, particularly Caucasians, to denote a certain level of sophistication. However, Japan's new-found self confidence has diminished their role since the young, unlike their predecessors, are much more sophisticated, widely travelled and well-versed in foreign brands and popular Western culture. The use of celebrities, both Japanese and Western is still prevalent. The hierarchical system in Japan has always endowed an authority figure with a certain amount of clout; the traditional approach to learning is one of emulation, a student copying the master. Hence celebrities are used to endorse anything from a brand of coffee, to a computer or a car. The copy may very well be void of any direct endorsement by the celebrity but the juxtaposition of the person with the product elevates the product to celebrity status. The intimation of a mood or feeling is adequate.

English has long been used in advertising, particularly in the naming of products: the number one selling sports drink is Pocari Sweat while a popular clothing brand is "A Bathing Ape". This might make little sense to the English speaker but the Japanese themselves do not always concern themselves with the meaning behind the names or phrases; it is the feel and look of the words that is important to them. The country has a history of assimilating foreign words into the Japanese language and making them their own. These words are referred to as "loan words" and are often relied upon in advertising copy as they can allow for a more casual tone. The Japanese have also long enjoyed a great predilection for puns and delight in the clever use of words. The nature of *kanji* (Chinese) characters, which have several pronunciations, allows for this play on words and is a tool often used in advertising.

As seen, changes are underfoot in Japan's new economy. Formality is slowly being replaced by the casual. In the youth oriented stores, epitomized by the Gap, sales people are more likely to great customers with a casual *konnichiwa* (hello) than the more polite "welcome" and some have even adopted a mute, nonchalant glance. Language is undergoing a quiet transition: English is intermingled freely with Japanese yet kanji and Japanese words are becoming vogue again. Meanwhile, television advertising has seen the breaking of one of its biggest taboos: the use of comparative advertising. Up until now, comparison with a competitor's product has generally been considered off limits. The breaking of this taboo however, like much else in advertising, is indicative of the slowly changing face and structure of Japan.

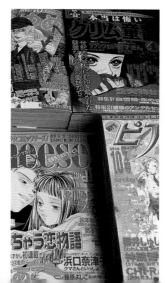

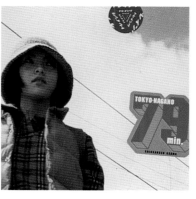

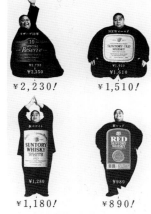

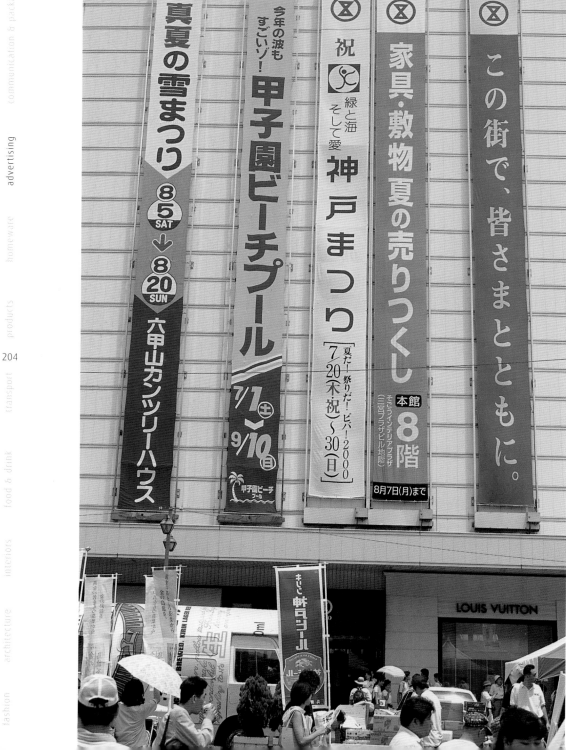

advertising banners cover a department store

communication & packaging

advertising

homeware

products

205

transport

food & drink

interiors

architecture

fashion

Banners were originally used by sparring clans in battle as a means of distinguishing themselves from the enemy. Today these banners remain and are a prevalent form of advertising particularly by department stores, hung from the sides of buildings to announce specific seasonal promotions and events, on the pavement beneath, mini banners promote a beer campaign. The corner *kushi-katsu* restaurant shown in the image below is typical of similar small establishments in that it is layered in advertising. The shop name is given in at least six different places: on a horizontal sign below the lantern, on the *noren* cloth that covers the door, on a vertical plaque hanging from the side of the building, on white paper lanterns above the noren, on the red lantern above the shop that lights up after dark, and, if that were not enough, a sign on top of the food display flashes the shop's name electronically. The red canopy advertises what there is to eat, a handwritten menu on a stand outside gives more details, while plastic samples of food in the window provide a visual menu. The availability of beer is apparent from the giant size glass of lager that lights up at night while the mythical figure of the *tanuki* (raccoon), a common sight outside such establishments, is armed with a flask of sake in perpetual pursuit of good drink and company.

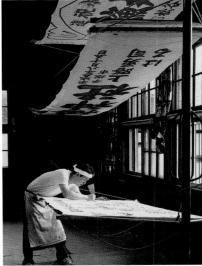

traditional banners being made

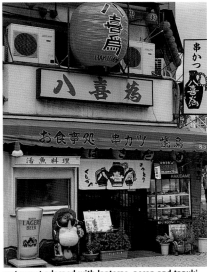

restaurant adorned with lanterns, noren and tanuki

communication & packaging

advertising

homeware

products

206

transport

food & drink

interiors

architecture

fashion

Noren cloth curtains are often hung over a restaurant or shop doorway. They serve a double purpose both advertising a business and indicating that a store is open when hung up or closed when taken down. They were especially useful in times when many stores operated out of the front of houses as there was little to indicate on the exterior of a building that it housed a business until the noren was hung out. The colourful noren to the right depicts the *kanji-yu,* meaning hot water and is used here as an abbreviated form for *sento* (public bathhouse). *Ryokan* (traditional inns) with their own hot spring pools hang noren to indicate which pool is for men and which is for women. Noren are not solely confined to businesses, and are sometimes hung in the home rather like a screen, serving as a subtle divider between the *genkan* (entrance) that connects to the outer world and the step up to the inner part of the house.

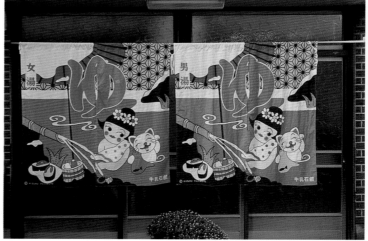

noren

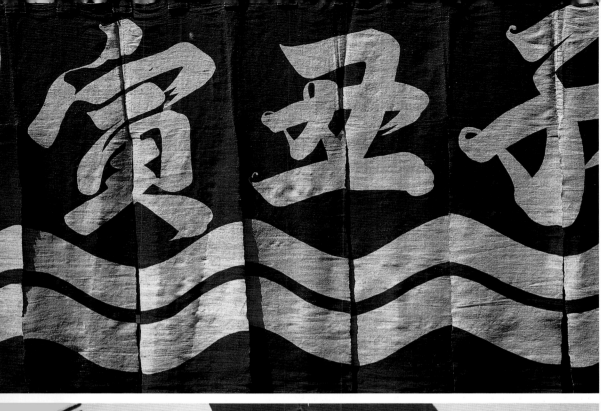

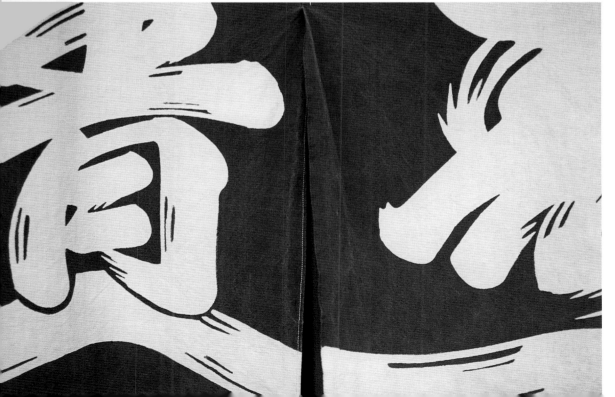

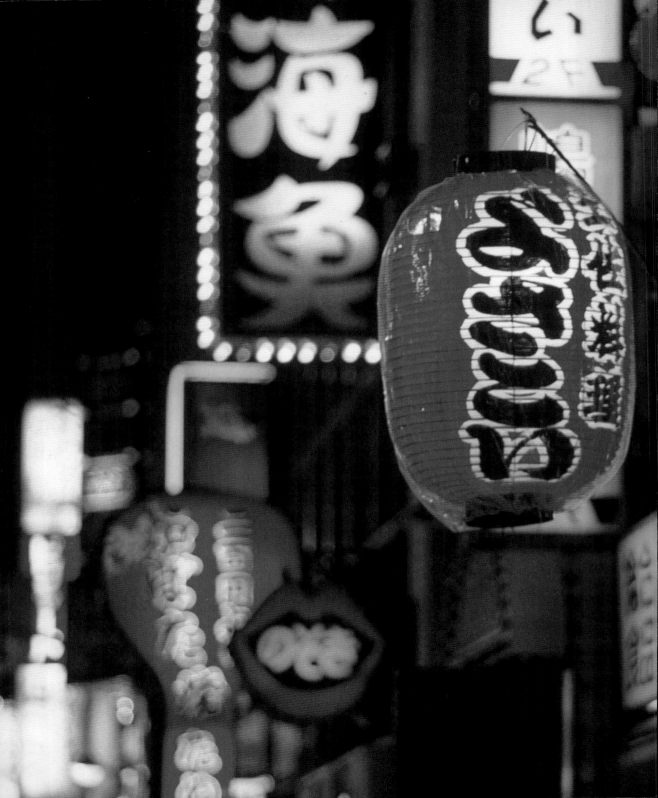

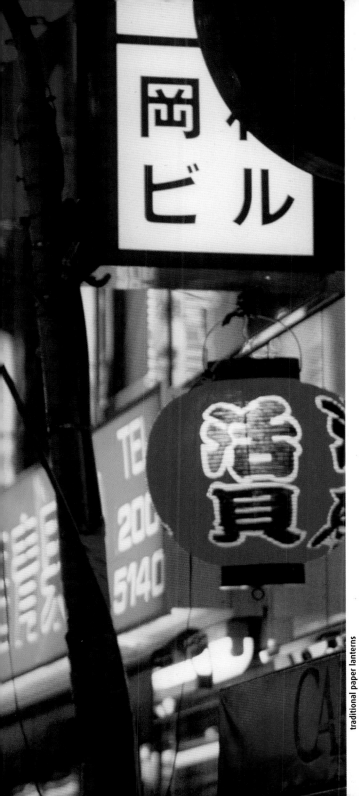

traditional paper lanterns

Early forms of lighting were usually constructed from wood, paper and candles. The *chochin* (paper lamp) evolved from this and is an ingenious design: concentric bamboo hoops form a framework which is covered in *washi* (handmade paper) and collapses flat when not in use. The washi is extremely durable and adds a translucent quality to the light. Paper lanterns come in a variety of shapes and sizes, red and white being the most common colours. Red lanterns often advertise drinking establishments and provide a warm, welcoming glow on a cold night. During festival time the famous geisha teahouses of Pontocho in Kyoto hang red lanterns decorated with their symbol, the plover. More colourful lanterns are used in summer to decorate beer gardens.

communication & packaging

advertising

homeware

products

209

transport

food & drink

interiors

architecture

fashion

communication & packaging

advertising

homeware

products

210

transport

food & drink

interiors

architecture

fashion

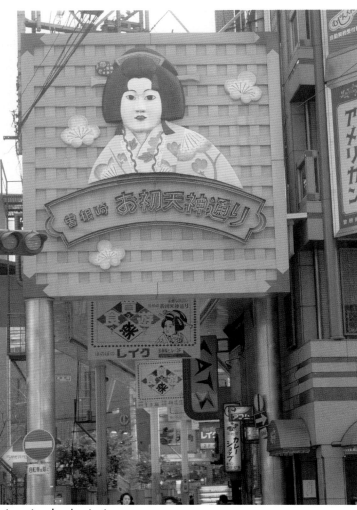

gateway to a shopping street

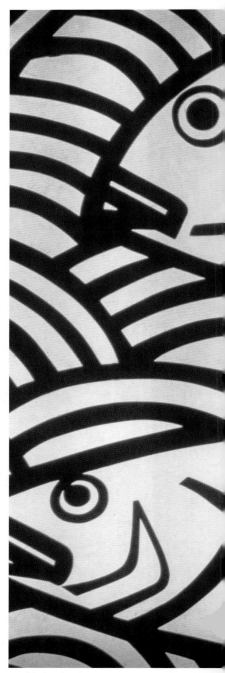

Just as the red *torii* gate to a shrine symbolizes entry from the outside world into the grounds of the shrine, so the entrance to shopping streets and arcades are marked through similar gate-like posts often adorned with logos.

Woodblock prints, made famous through the works of such artists as Hiroshige and Hokusai, are evocative of the Edo period. Food packaging and shop signs often use the bold, sharp, contrasting lines of the woodblock print style for advertising, capitalizing on its folksy, down-to-earth appeal.

woodblock-style prints

communication & packaging

advertising

homeware

products

211

transport

food & drink

interiors

architecture

fashion

communication & packaging

advertising

homeware

products

212

transport

food & drink

interiors

architecture

fashion

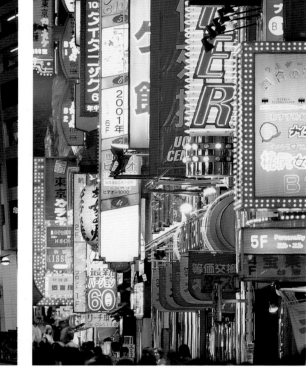

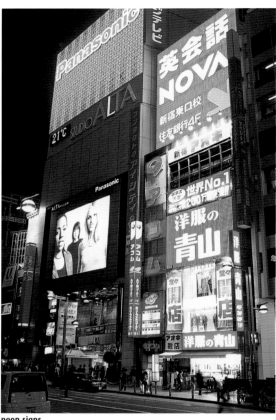

neon signs

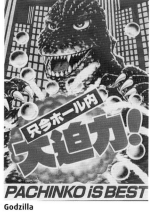

Godzilla

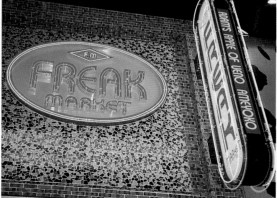

use of English in signage

communication & packaging

advertising

homeware

products

213

transport

food & drink

interiors

architecture

fashion

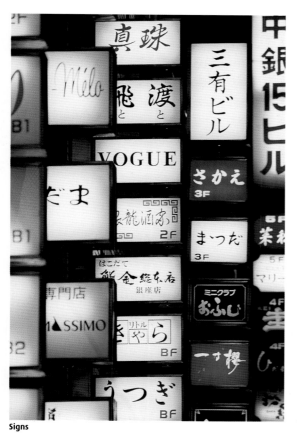

Signs

The density of Japan's urban areas means development tends to expand vertically as opposed to horizontally. As a result, advertising also extends up with layers of neon-lit signs indicating the business on each floor of a building. Japan's ability to adapt and integrate other cultures into their own is reflected in its myriad forms of advertising. As with Japanese magazines, a combination of Japanese *kanji* (characters), *romaji* (phonetic symbols) are mixed freely with English on the neon signs with some signs reading traditionally from top to bottom while others read from left to right.

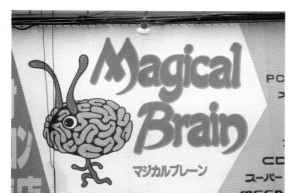

English in advertising is used in a rather liberal fashion. Famous brand names like Vogue and Dunhill are adopted by hostess clubs hoping to cash in on the cachet of their namesakes. While creative use of the English language may prove a selling point in Japan, it may make little sense at all to the native speaker in some cases.

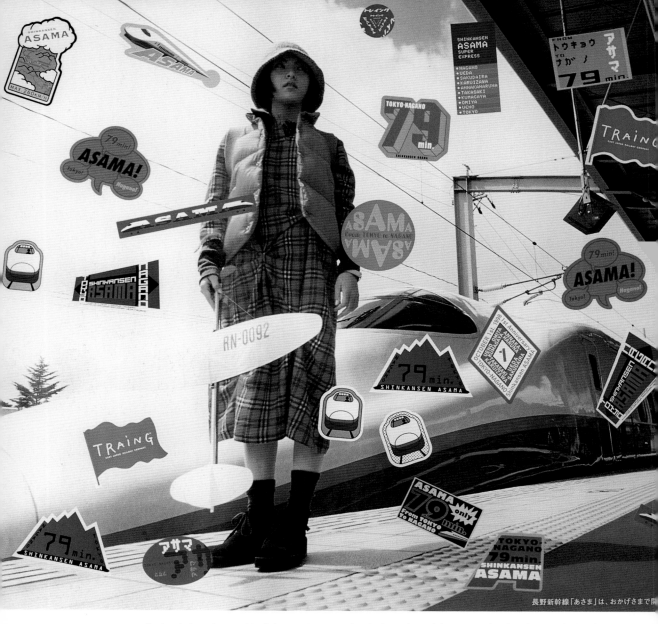

長野新幹線「あさま」は、おかげさまで開

Tourism in Japan began with pilgrimages. Townspeople visited temples and shrines armed with stickers inscribed with their name, which they would then stick on the temples and shrines. This custom is still practiced by devout pilgrims today. The East Japan Railways advertisement shown above pays homage to this tradition using contemporary stickers to advertise their Asama Shinkansen service between Tokyo and Nagano. Japan's railway companies have long used seasonal imagery to promote travel throughout the year. With the aim of luring urbanites into the countryside, idyllic rural scenes are accompanied by copy that is intended to invoke a certain nostalgia and longing for the country, far removed from urban reality.

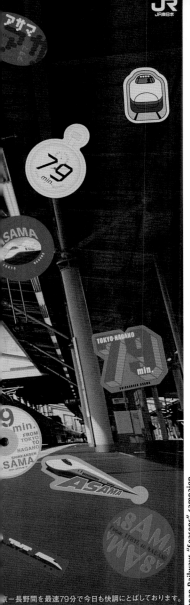

Japan Railways "Seasons" campaign

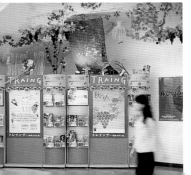

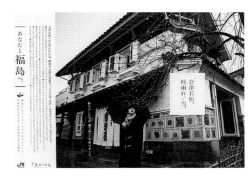

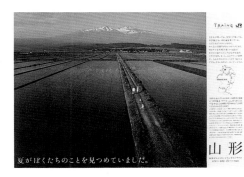

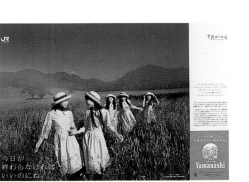

communication & packaging

advertising

homeware

215

products

transport

food & drink

interiors

architecture

fashion

communication & packaging

advertising

homeware

products

216

transport

food & drink

interiors

architecture

fashion

The Iichiko ads are part of a successful, long-running campaign that discretely features a bottle of iichiko (a spirit) placed within a larger vista. The copy is simple and ethereal like a line from a haiku, quietly evoking a mood for something even bigger. Through understatement, the advertisement subtly succeeds in standing out, in that Japanese "less is more" fashion. While the Iichiko ad quietly announces its presence, the Nissin Cup Noodle ad screams for attention. Packing a strong visual punch, the Nissin advertisement works on the basis that what you see is what you get, with its simple English copy "Hungry?".

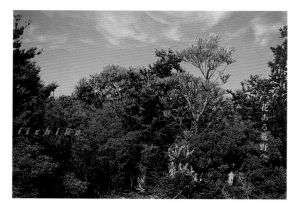

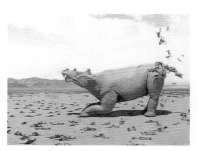

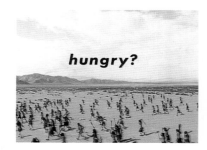

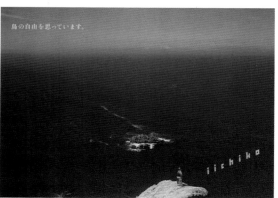

Iichiko advertisements

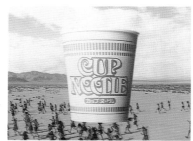

Nissin Cup Noodle advertisement

Konishiki, shown in this Suntory whisky advertisement, is now retired but is one of Japan's most famous sumo wrestlers. Here he uses his sumo size body to effectively recreate the shapes of bottles for Suntory's line of whiskies.

度目の酒税改正
めでとうございます気分。
れをきっかけに、
もあなたも

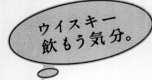
ウイスキー
飲もう気分。

てことにしちゃい
せんか気分。

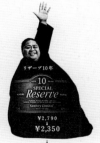
¥3,570
¥3,180
¥3,000!

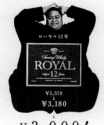
¥2,790
¥2,350
¥2,230!

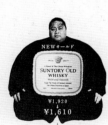
¥1,920
¥1,610
¥1,510!

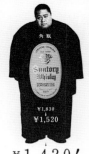
¥1,830
¥1,520
¥1,420!

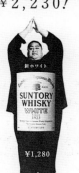
¥1,280
¥1,180!

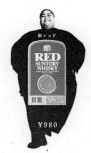
¥980
¥890!

WE-SU
SUNTOR

ウイスキー史上最高！気分のプレゼントネ。

に付いている点数シールを集めてください。30点から500点までの点数に応じて合計31種類の"ウイスキー飲もう気分"グッズ
希望のものを、応募者全員にかならず差し上げます。詳しいプレゼント内容、応募方法は、各製品に首かけされているリーフレ
さい。対象製品の点数シールは、例えばローヤル12年/10点、NEWオールド/6点、新レッド/3点（レギュラーサイズの場合）
切りも：平成10年10月31日 当日酒印有効 ※応募は20歳以上の方に限らせていただきます。※装品の写真は実物と多少異なる場合があります。

Konishiki Suntory whisky advert

communication & packaging

advertising

homeware

products

218

transport

food & drink

interiors

architecture

fashion

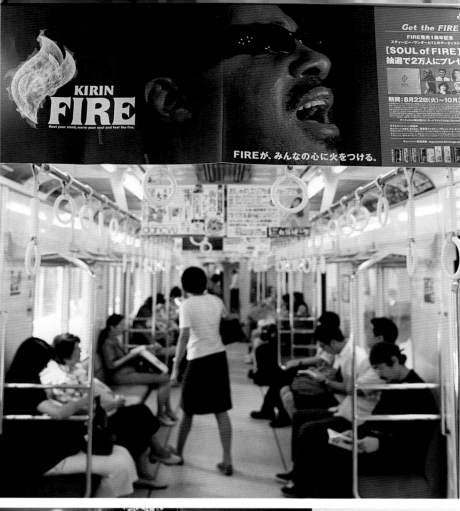

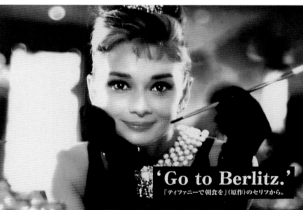

'Go to Berlitz.'

ずーっと昔から、
語学習得の代名詞。
ベルリッツ

■ 教育訓練給付制度 指定講座あり。
　受講料の80%（上限20万円）を国が支給（一定条件あり）。

■ 英語、フランス語、ドイツ語、中国語等、10数カ国語の
　レッスンをご用意。

信頼と先端の教授法　ベルリッツ

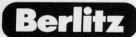

www.berlitz.com

communication & packaging

advertising

homeware

products

219

transport

food & drink

interiors

architecture

fashion

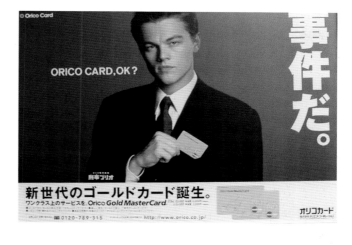

Advertisers in Japan have long depended upon celebrity advertising, in particular the use of Westerners, to endorse a product. Sharon Stone, Bruce Willis and Meg Ryan appear in Japanese commercials with a stipulation in their contracts that the commercials will not be shown overseas, as the Japanese perception of a celebrity is often quite different from their Western image. For example here Leonardo Di Caprio appears earnest in a business suit promoting a gold Mastercard while Cameron Diaz, less sex symbol and more saccharine, promotes English lessons. Posters in trains fill carriage walls and hang suspended from the ceiling. The Stevie Wonder poster opposite promotes a brand of canned coffee drinks called Fire, the drinks appearing discretely at the side. As with many posters, a mixture of English and Japanese is used. The tag line is in English, "Kirin FIRE, Rest your mind, warm your soul and feel the fire" while translated, the Japanese copy reads, "FIRE sets everyone's heart ablaze".

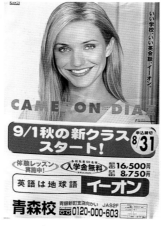

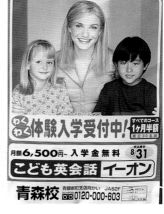

communication & packaging

advertising

homeware

products

220

transport

food & drink

interiors

architecture

fashion

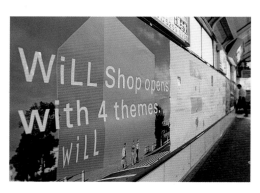

The Will campaign is symbolized by the orange cube that has become the logo of Will products. The campaign is unique in that it is a collaborative effort among several major corporations to collectively brand specifically designed products in a way that will appeal to the lucrative, yet increasingly fickle market of those in their late twenties. Toyota has designed the Will Vi car; Asahi has produced a beer; Matsushita, a retro-looking fridge and a sleek computer; Kokuyo, office furniture and stationery. In addition there are Will hair products, chocolate and even Will tours. Most of the products feature the clean Will packaging: a white background with an orange cube.

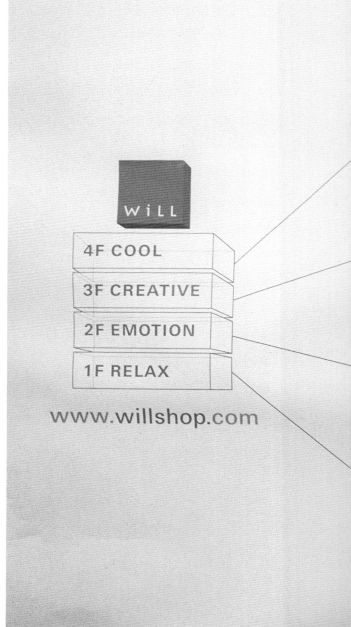

Will advertising campaign

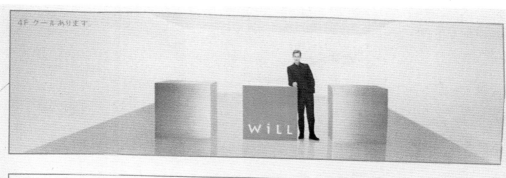

4F クールあります。

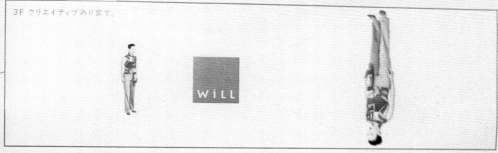

3F クリエイティブあります。

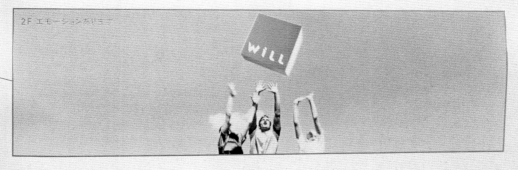

2F エモーションあります

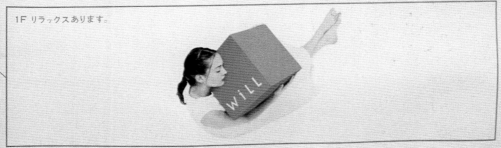

1F リラックスあります。

communication & packaging

advertising

homeware

products

221

transport

food & drink

interiors

architecture

fashion

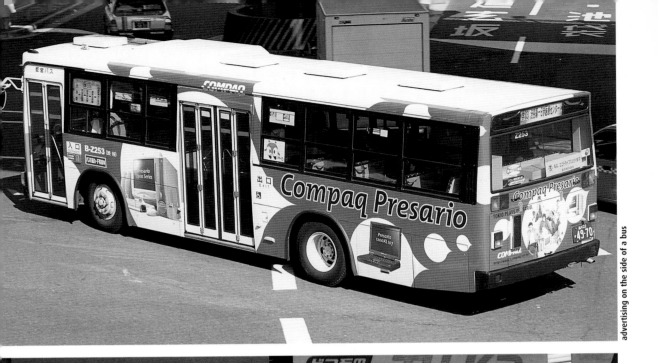

advertising on the side of a bus

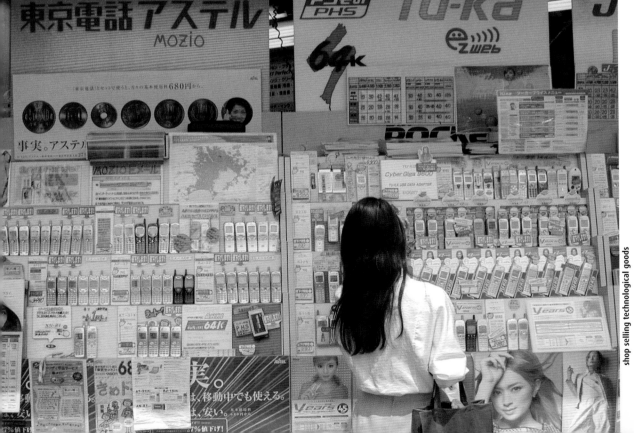

shop selling technological goods

communication & packaging

advertising

homeware

products

223

transport

food & drink

interiors

architecture

fashion

Saturated in advertising, multimedia has become an integral part of the urban landscape. Several television screens at one of Japan's busiest street crossings can cause chaos when broadcasting a major news event as all eyes become riveted to the screens. Screens vary in size from the enormous ones adorning the sides of buildings to more discrete ones embedded in walls or, as in the image below, a lamp post. There is nothing of the "less is more" philosophy in the advertising here. The stand promoting cellular phones and services, represents the flip side of Japanese austerity where a bazaar mentality rules and goods are displayed to the maximum with colourful and vibrant imagery competing with text-laden data. Seen on a larger scale, such displays are emblematic of the nation's cities with its multi-layering of billboards, banners, TV screens and shop signage. The pictographic nature of kanji has given the Japanese an acute appreciation for the visual which may account for the immense popularity of manga shown on the mural. These comic-like stories have a cross-generational appeal and have cultivated their own form of visual shorthand language in rather the same manner that icons have now been adopted by cellular phone users to expedite their e-mails.

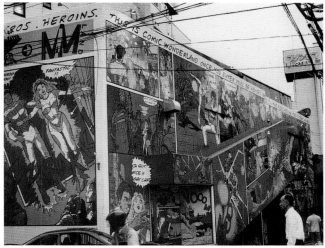

Comic World, Tokyo

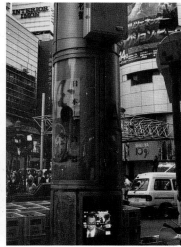

television within telegraph pole

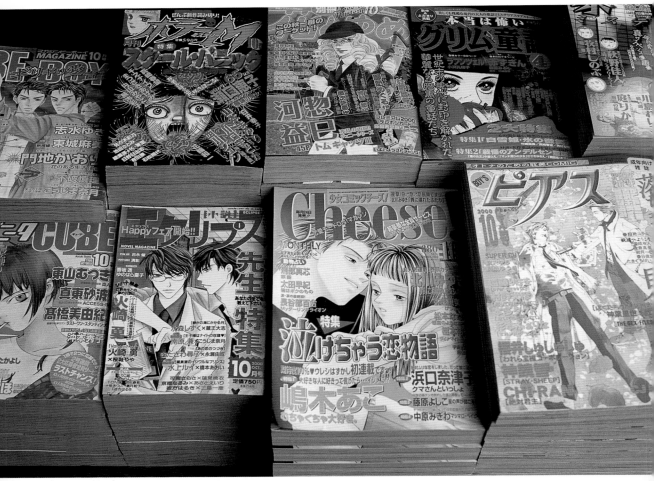

Japanese magazines

Japan is awash with magazines from inch-thick manga comics, to an elaborate array of magazines catering to every sector of the market. Magazine names tend to be in English: *Brutus* is a popular men's magazine while *Cutie, CanCan, Fruits, ChouChou, Zipper, Wink up, Potato* and *Cawaii* are all titles aimed at the young female market. The latter, *Cawaii*, is a play on words of the Japanese word for cute, *kawaii*. As with other forms of media, magazines tend to use English for titles and Japanese for the main body of text. Reading tends to be in the traditional manner with the magazine being read from right to left, although design dictates whether columns be read vertically from top to bottom and right to left as is customary or in the Western manner horizontally from left to right.

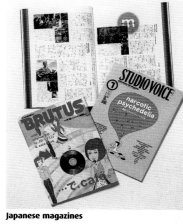

Japanese magazines

225

communication & packaging

advertising

homeware

products

226

transport

food & drink

interiors

architecture

fashion

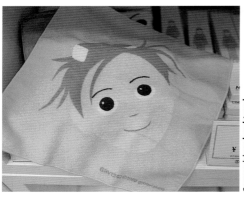

Groovevisions hand towel

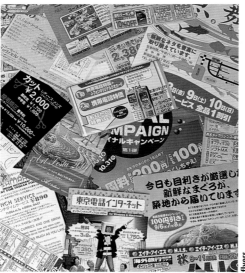

flyers

advertising on chopstick wrappers

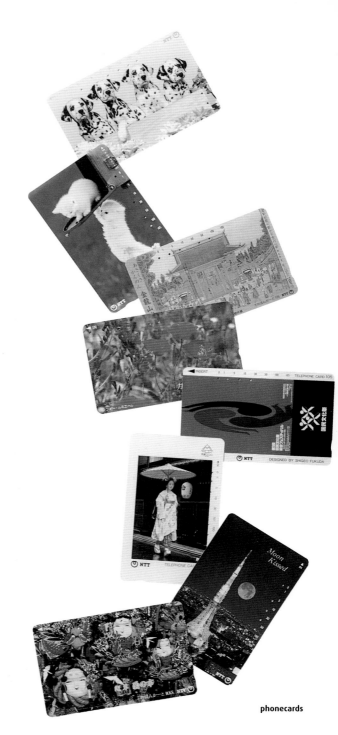

phonecards

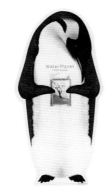

The colourful fliers and handbills that exist today are a legacy of the Edo period when multicoloured woodblock prints were used to advertise businesses. Striking woodblock handbills have given way to contemporary computer-generated, graphic-laden images and text, promoting anything from internet services and curry rice to less salubrious offerings. Tissue packs, handed out free at major stations, are also a popular form of advertising and seem to be especially favoured by insurance companies. The Edo period also saw the use of *tenugui* as a means of advertising with the name of a business printed on the material. This tradition has been continued and is particularly prevalent among onsen where hand towels are issued featuring the name of the hot spring replete with its telephone number. Ryokan often feature their name on the yukata that bathers sometimes wear around town as they go from one hot spring to another, while traditional *uchiwa* (paper fans) and old-fashioned paper umbrellas are also used for advertising purposes.

tissues

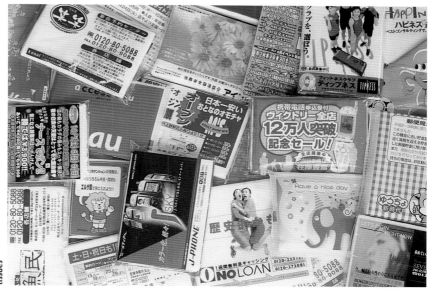

hand towels

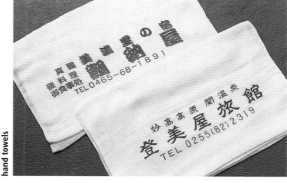

advertising

honeware

products

228

transport

food & drink

interiors

architecture

fashion

communication & packaging

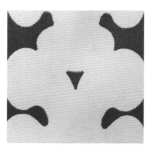

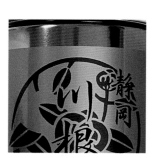

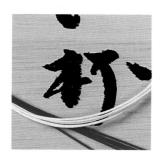

Symbols and patterns are prolific in Japan. Recurring themes and images provide an underlying sense of order and symmetry to an outwardly frenetic world: vegetables impeccably displayed in neat bundles, bamboo fences tied with string in perfectly aligned knots, red *torii* gates leading in succession up to a shrine. These repetitive images are woven into the fabric of daily life and form the basis of a nation that is long accustomed to visual forms of communication.

Appearance in Japan is everything; form comes before function, or at least is of equal worth. The writing of *haiku* (traditional 17-syllable verse) is judged not solely on content, but on the overall package – the style of the calligraphy and also the way it is presented. This philosophy has provided the Japanese with a framework of rules and social etiquette that has long governed behaviour. Traditionally, gifts are presented in a certain manner in the same way that food is eaten in a prescribed order and the kimono worn in a particular way. It was once common practice when giving a gift to use only white paper, a symbol of purity. Strict guidelines decreed that the paper should be folded so that the right-hand edge extended over to the left edge of the package. Only on sombre occasions was the wrapping ever reversed. *Mizuhiki*, paper cords in felicitous colours of red, white, silver and gold were used to hold the paper together with black and white cords reserved for funerals; attached to the package was a *noshi* – a long thin strip of abalone. Today such formal etiquette is not widely practised although mizuhiki are still used to tie gifts and abalone has been replaced with noshi made from folded paper or on more casual occasions, a graphic image.

This copious attention to detail is an underlying tenet of Japanese culture and can be seen everywhere from the crisply suited salarymen to the rigorously raked Zen gardens. It is also evident in the everyday packaging of goods. No matter how insignificant an item, the same meticulous level of care goes into its packaging: bold colours and detailed drawings on cheap packets of sweets and chocolate, biscuits in a packet with each one individually wrapped or a bento box with a tiny plastic fish and minute red cap filled with a single serving of soy sauce. Japan is a country where

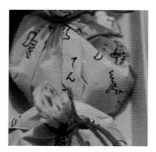

communication & packaging

advertising

homeware

products

229

transport

food & drink

interiors

architecture

fashion

small is beautiful. Sipping size portions of beer are sold in miniature cans. Child-size cartons of liquid yoghurt come in tiny tetrapak containers with a straw attached. Cheap one-size servings of sake are sold in plastic bottles with a top that cleverly doubles as a sake cup. Large, discount-sized goods and bulk items are irrelevant in a country where there is so little space.

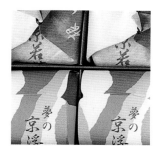

In general, Japanese companies spend far more on packaging than their Western counterparts and the Japanese consumer pays a premium for this. In return they can expect innovative packaging that is continually being modified and updated with new materials. This is of course, the country that invented the instant "cup noodle". Containers and bottles are perpetually fashioned into new shapes and beauty is viewed as an integral part of function. Nowhere is the emphasis on packaging and presentation more evident than in department stores, renowned for their lavish wrapping of gifts. Exquisitely packaged individual cakes sold in a decorative *washi* (handmade paper) covered box, will be further wrapped in the store's own paper by a deft shop assistant trained in the ways of wrapping. Wrapping is an art form itself and invariably relies upon skillful folding of paper using only paper cord or ribbon. This tape free approach to wrapping has its roots in *origami*, which literally means "folding of paper". Origami is a skill that has been passed down through the ages and the Japanese carry it on to this day. Sit in a Japanese restaurant where there are no chopstick rests and someone will soon be folding their chopstick wrapper into one. Folding and tucking are inherent to the Japanese, evidence of which is found in all aspects of the culture – the folds of a *hakama* (part of male kimono), food wrapped in leaves, books that unfold like an accordion and paper tucked into the folds of a kimono to serve as a plate for sweets in a tea ceremony.

The recent closure of some department stores and Japan's ailing economy has meant less money for packaging and emphasis is now being placed upon more environmentally conscious products. Since the Nara period (705–794), the Japanese have been using *furoshiki* an eco-friendly and resourceful way of wrapping and carrying goods. Furoshiki consist of a square piece of cloth, usually cotton or silk that is folded over an item then tied diagonally at the corners to make a handle and can be used to wrap and carry anything from a melon or a bottle of wine to a futon. Although the carrier bag has taken over, furoshiki are still used today. They were also used as an early form of advertising by merchants to display their crests.

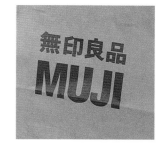

Crests first emerged in the Heian period (794–1185) and were adopted by courtesans. Later they appeared on the banners of sparring warriors as a means of identification. The symbols used represent common themes from nature such as plants and animals. During the Edo period

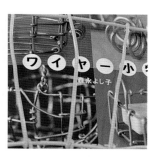

crests became widespread and all sections of society began to wear them on their clothing as they still do today. The symbols and patterns that adorn the Japanese landscape are part of a culture that loves a readily identifiable logo. Family crests on kimonos, salarymen wearing corporate logo pins, restaurant signage on chopstick wrappers, motif-embossed talismen from shrines and even bags sporting Louis Vuitton and Prada logos are all testament to a country driven by the visual.

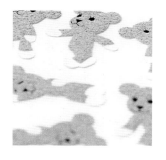

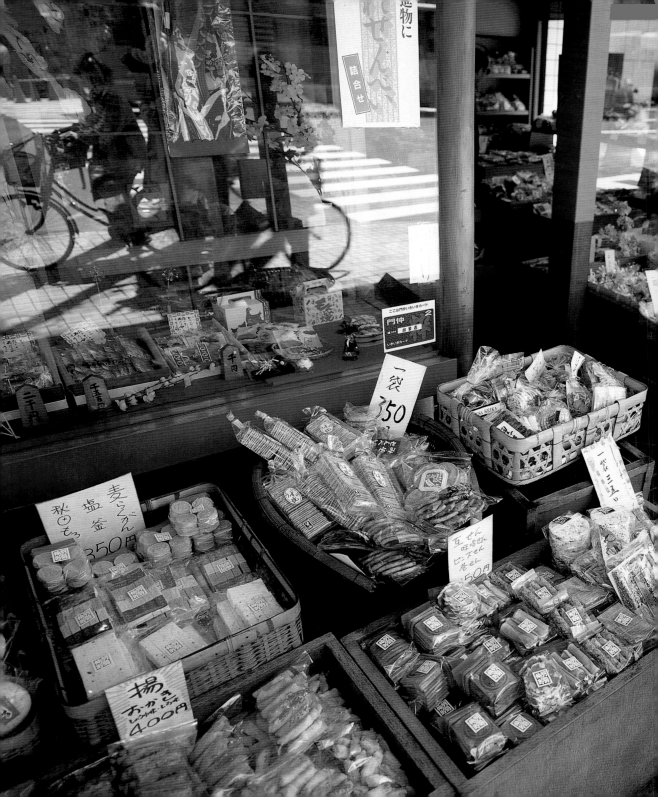

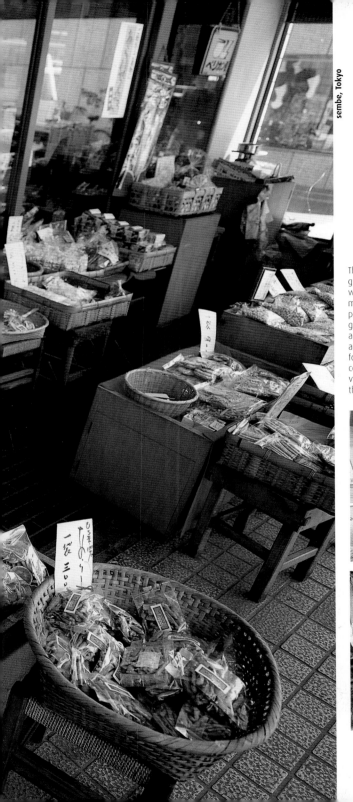

communication & packaging

advertising

homeware

products

transport

231

food & drink

interiors

architecture

fashion

sembe, Tokyo

This old fashioned *sembe* (rice cracker) store displays the price of its goods on wooden trays in the window. Like many small shops, wares are displayed on the street as if they were selling goods at market. Fruit sold in department stores commands outrageously high prices, particularly melons and peaches, which are usually bought as gifts as opposed to personal consumption. Perfectly formed melons and large apples are individually wrapped then packaged in a box appropriate for gift giving. In the days before refrigeration many foods were either smoked or hung to dry and hanging is still a common means of storage and display today. At one time street vendors would hawk goods tied to the end of a pole and slung over the shoulder.

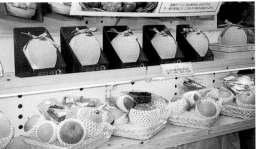

packaged fruit

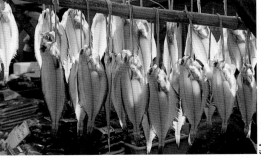

fish

communication & packaging

advertising

homeware

products

232

transport

food & drink

interiors

architecture

fashion

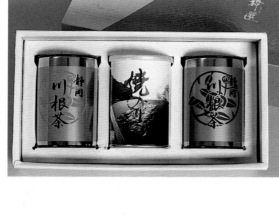

o-seibo tea and seaweed set

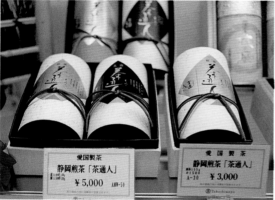

tea set

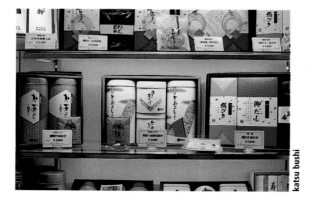

katsu bushi

communication & packaging

advertising

homeware

products

233

transport

food & drink

interiors

architecture

fashion

The Westernization of Japan, spurred by department store promotions of events such as Christmas and Valentine's Day, has seen the introduction of gift giving on these occasions especially among the young. Traditionally, however, Japan's two main gift-giving seasons are *o-chugen* in July and *o-seibo* in December when gifts are given those to whom one has been indebted throughout the year. Consultants at department stores are made available to dispense advice on the fine art of deciding the appropriate level of gift to be given. Carefully decorated boxes display suitable gifts such as tea, seaweed and dried fish flakes. Elegant packaging is not solely confined to gifts. Bento boxes wrapped in fabric-like paper are tied like *furoshiki* while bamboo leaves are tied around rice balls.

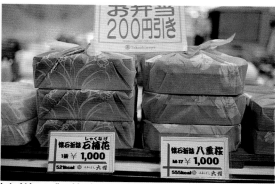

kaiseki bento (lunchbox) wrapped in washi

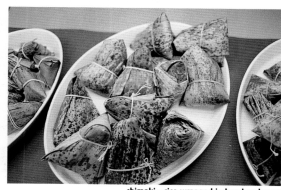

chimaki – rice wrapped in bamboo leaves

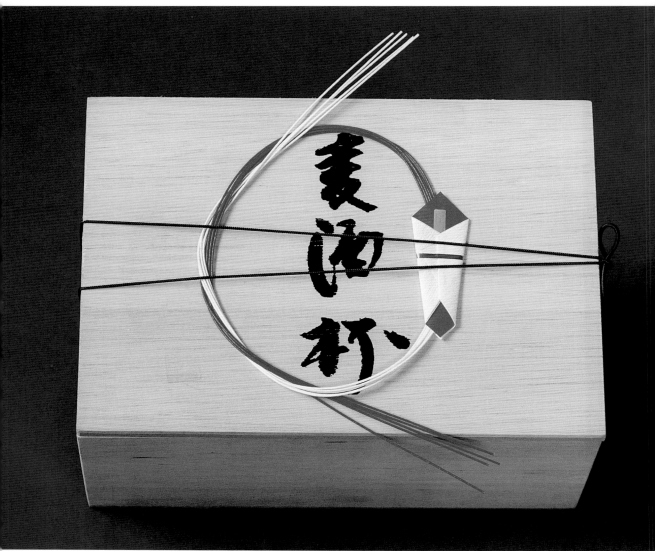

mizuhiki

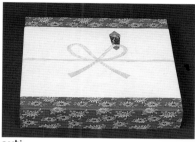

noshi

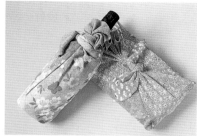

furoshiki

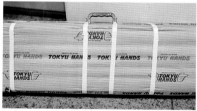

packaging from Tokyu Hands department store

Mizuhiki are paper cords that are used to wrap congratulatory envelopes and gifts. Although some mizuhiki are now made by machine and come in a wide range of colours, many are still hand dyed by families who have passed the craft down through generations. The knot tied in a mizuhiki symbolizes the bond between people and over the years the tying of the knot has become an elaborate art form with knots fashioned into butterflies, cranes and bamboo leaves. The folded red and white paper to the right of the knot is the *noshi* that at one time was a strip of dried abalone – fish has always been deemed a valued gift in Shintoism. A printed sheet of paper depicting the mizuhiki and noshi is commonly used for less formal gifts. Tying and knotting are an integral part of Japanese culture. Lucky paper fortunes bought at shrines are tied to trees, furoshiki are knotted into portable bags and even department stores tie goods together with great precision, as in the case of Tokyu Hands (left), adding a green plastic handle to facilitate carrying.

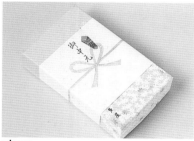

ochugen

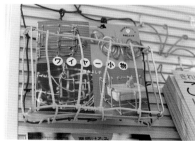

wire packaging

In a country where form is so important, it is no surprise that the proffering of a gift is as much about appearance as it is to do with the actual content. Individual cakes are wrapped in exquisitely dyed *washi* (handmade paper) and each perfectly knotted illustrate the importance paid to detail in packaging and presentation.

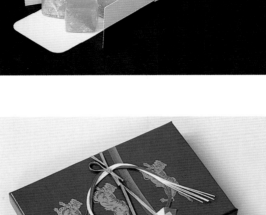

bontan candy

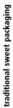

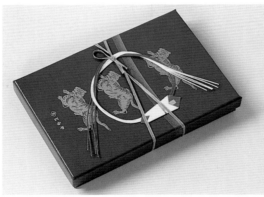

traditional sweet packaging

wagashi – sweets wrapped in washi

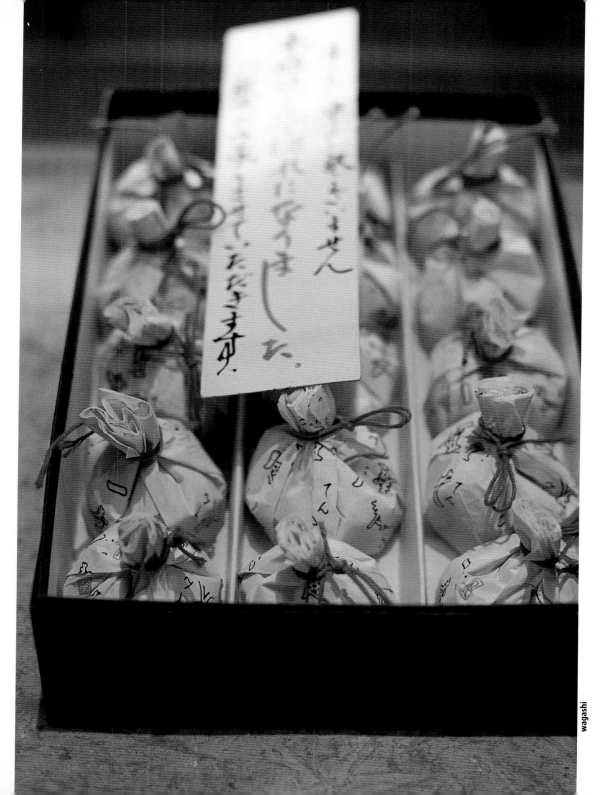

communication & packaging

advertising

homeware

products

237

transport

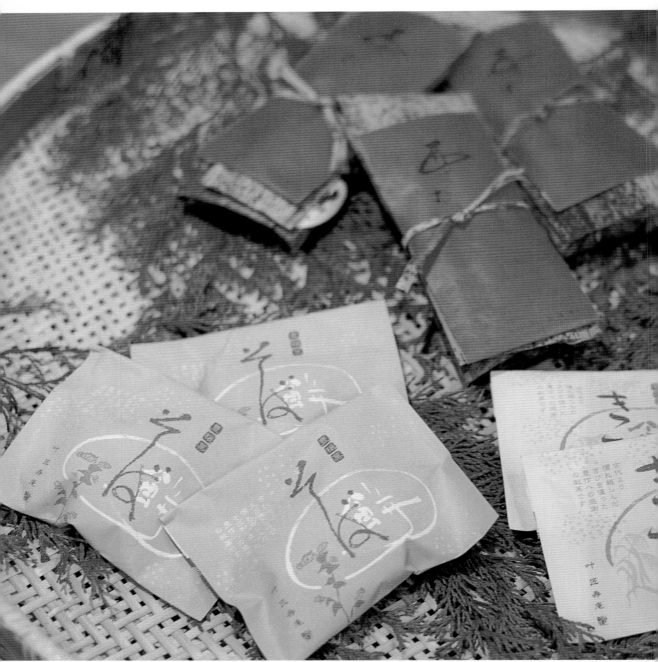

mochi

communication & packaging

advertising

homeware

products

239

transport

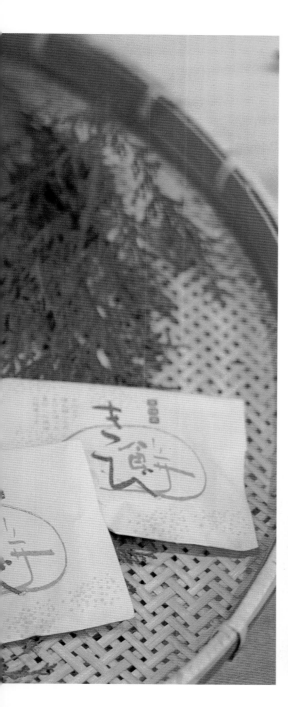

While Western packaging of goods tends to focus on the box or container, Japanese packaging often will wrap each item individually like these *mochi* sweets (left). Even children's sweets enjoy great attention to detail as can be seen in these caramels packaged in boxes decorated as dice.

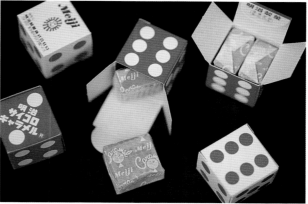

Cyclo Ame caramels

communication & packaging

advertising

homeware

products

240

transport

food & drink

interiors

architecture

fashion

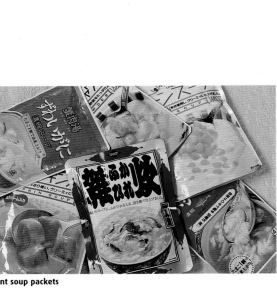

instant soup packets

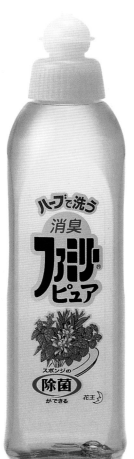

Family Pure detergent

The boil in the bag soup packets cater not only to convenience but are eco-friendly as the contents are printed on the outside of the pack reducing the need for extra packaging. These packets are also used as refillable packs for oils, dressings and even shampoos. As space is a premium in Japan consumers tend to prefer smaller-sized goods often in cute colours such as pink or peach such as this washing up liquid bottle. Foreign products are repackaged for the domestic market with Japanese names such as *Chocowa* and *Corn Frosty* as shown opposite. An absence of storage space and the serving of generally smaller portions means the large discount size packages available in the West are typically not for sale in Japan.

communication & packaging

advertising

homeware

products

transport

food & drink

interiors

architecture

fashion

241

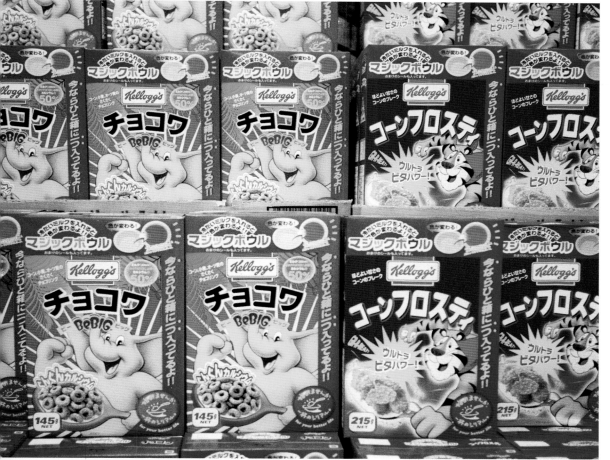

breakfast cereals repackaged for the Japanese market

communication & packaging

advertising

homeware

products

242

transport

food & drink

interiors

architecture

fashion

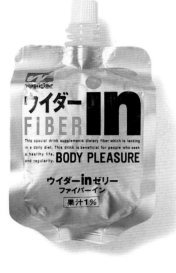

Fiber-in drink

As the name states, "Fiber-In" is a jelly like drink that is meant to supplement a diet with extra fibre. It comes in a silver pouch pack with a white cap that when unscrewed allows the jelly to be squeezed out as you would toothpaste.

Drinking whisky became popular in the postwar period encouraged by domestic production. Early bottles attempted to emulate the whisky of Scotland and the heritage it bestowed upon the product. In recent years whisky makers have tried to widen their appeal from middle-aged salarymen drinking *mizu-wari* (whisky with ice and water) to a younger market, through the introduction of simple packaging and generic shaped bottles.

Will Beer's simple labelling is part of a larger promotion of different Will products, and is designed to look more like a fashion accessory than a hearty beer beverage.

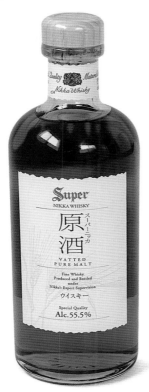

whisky

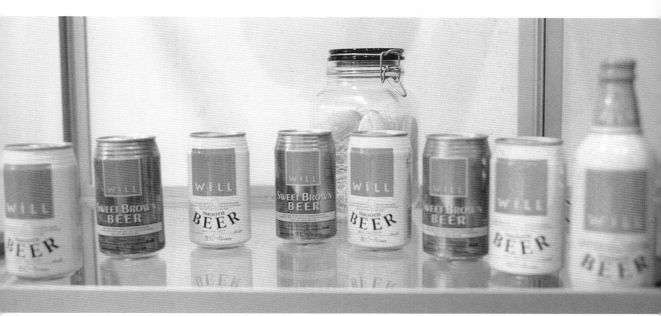

Will beer

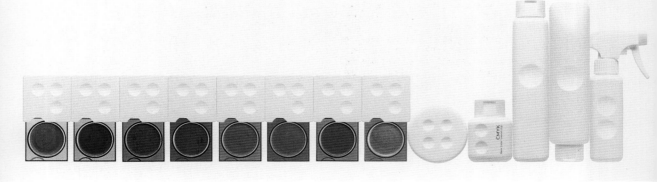

CMYK make-up

communication & packaging

advertising

homeware

products

245

transport

food & drink

interiors

architecture

fashion

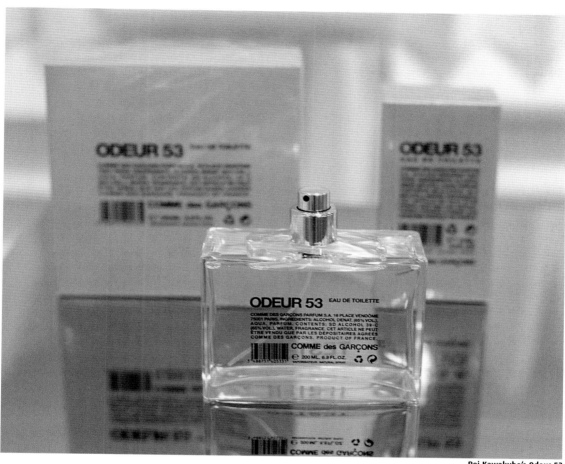

Rei Kawakubo's Odeur 53

The stark white containers of CMYK's hair and make up products (opposite) stand out due to their minimal packaging and noticeable lack of logos and printed matter. Comme des Garçons' eau de toilette, Odeur 53, like many of Rei Kawakubo's products, flies in the face of conventional wisdom. There is no defining product name but instead an "Odeur" number on the side of a minimalist bottle where the contents of the package are also listed replete with barcode. Her previous perfume came in a sealed plastic bottle with a curved base that did not stand up.

communication & packaging

advertising

homeware

products

246

transport

food & drink

interiors

architecture

fashion

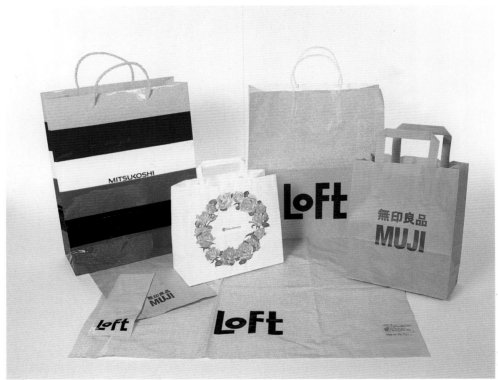

carrier bags

Japanese fashion designers bring the same level of detail to their packaging as they do to their clothing design and store interiors. The bag for Issey Miyake's A-POC line mirrors his new line of clothing. A flat thermally sealed rectangular piece of silver material (bottom right) has a push out top that enables the package to be opened while the outer edge becomes the shoulder strap. Yohji Yamamoto's blue crepe bags with black lining (top right) have no handle but are folded and held together by a black elastic cord. Mujirushi Rhoyin whose generic brown bag (above) is printed both in Japanese and the abbreviated "Muji" in English demonstrates the company's policy of using recycled materials and minimal packaging.

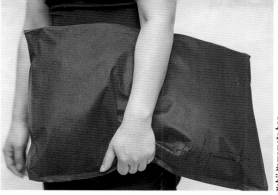

Yohji Yamamoto bag

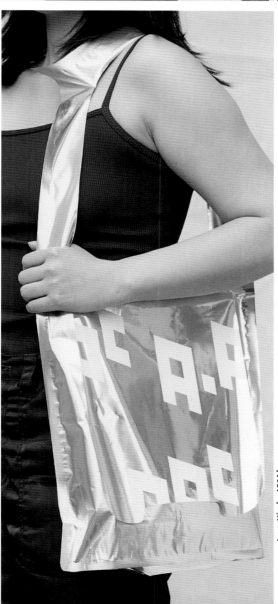

Issey Miyake APOC bag

communication & packaging

advertising

homeware

products

247

transport

food & drink

interiors

architecture

fashion

advertising

homeware

products

248

transport

food & drink

interiors

architecture

fashion

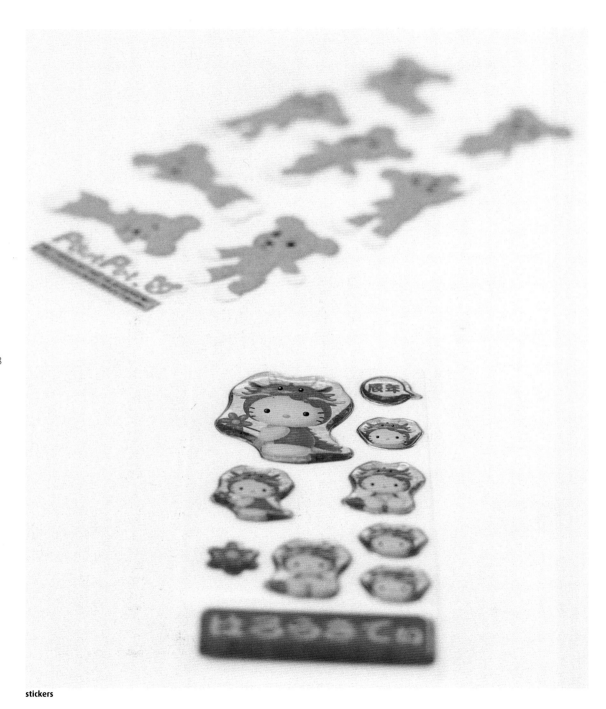

stickers

communication & packaging

advertising

homeware

products

transport

249

food & drink

interiors

architecture

fashion

Stickers are usually associated with Japanese schoolgirls who adorn envelopes, notebooks and even cellphones with miniature pandas, daruma and other cute figures. Stickers are believed to have originated in the Heian period when prayers and names were written on wooden tablets then hung at the temple gate during pilgrimages. Over time the tablets became paper stickers with the name of the pilgrim. Old name stickers can still be found at temples across the country, while some pilgrims today still carry their own stickers. Post Pet, the pink teddy sticker is in fact an email software pet that adorns messages. It grows like an animal and like any other virtual pet, needs to be fed and looked after.

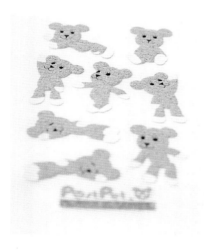

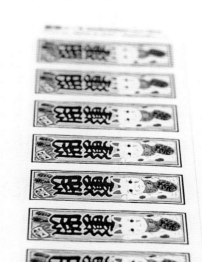

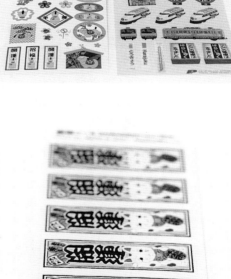

communication & packaging

advertising

homeware

products

250

transport

food & drink

interiors

architecture

fashion

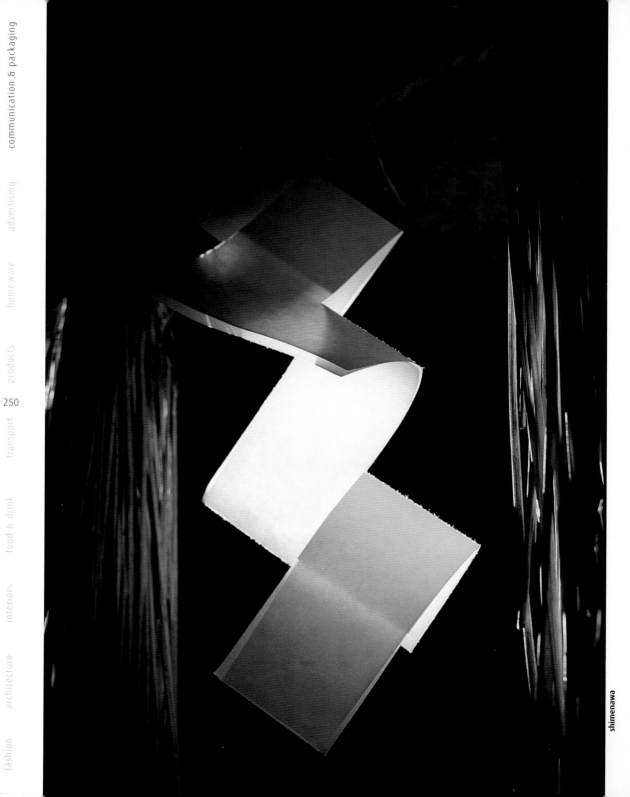

shimenawa

communication & packaging

advertising

homeware

products

251

transport

food & drink

interiors

architecture

fashion

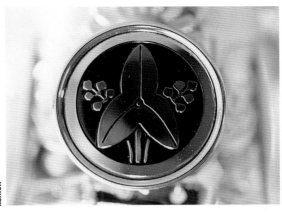

kamon

Shimenawa are the sacred straw ropes hung at Shinto shrines that are believed to prevent evil from entering. Made from rice straw they are also hung around trees and other objects deemed to be sacred. Suspended from the straw rope is a folded piece of symbolic white paper. The origins of *origami* are believed to come from the folding of paper used in Shinto ceremonies.

Kamon, family crests, reflect Japan's predeliction for the pictorial. The country's most illustrious crest is the chrysanthemum with sixteen petals, reserved solely for use by the Imperial Family.

communication & packaging

advertising

homeware

products

252

transport

food & drink

interiors

architecture

fashion

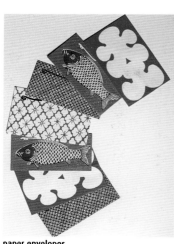

paper envelopes

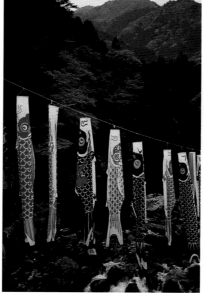

carp streamers

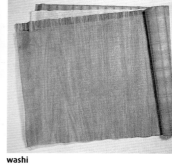

washi

Washi is extremely durable and versatile despite its opaque appearance. It has served a multitude of functions in Japanese culture and was once used for clothing and cooking utensils. Today it is still used for the making of lanterns, fans, shoji screens and fusuma in addition to cards and scrolls.

In lieu of Christmas cards, the Japanese send New Year greeting cards to friends and colleagues. In recent years, some have dispensed with cards altogether opting to send an email greeting , while many others choose to have customized cards printed. A handwritten, New Year greeting in calligraphy on a washi decorated card is still, however, deemed to be the most courteous greeting.

communication & packaging

advertising

homeware

products

253

transport

food & drink

interiors

architecture

fashion

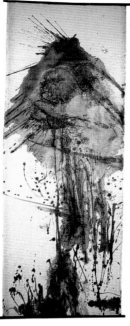

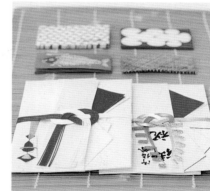

stationery

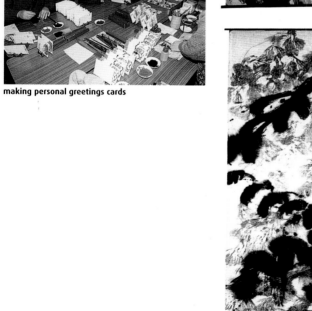

making personal greetings cards

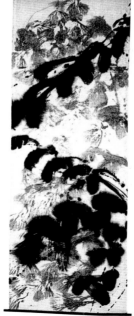

washi scrolls

index

communication & packaging

advertising

homeware

products

transport

food & drink

interiors

architecture

fashion

254